D0679369
WITHDRAWN

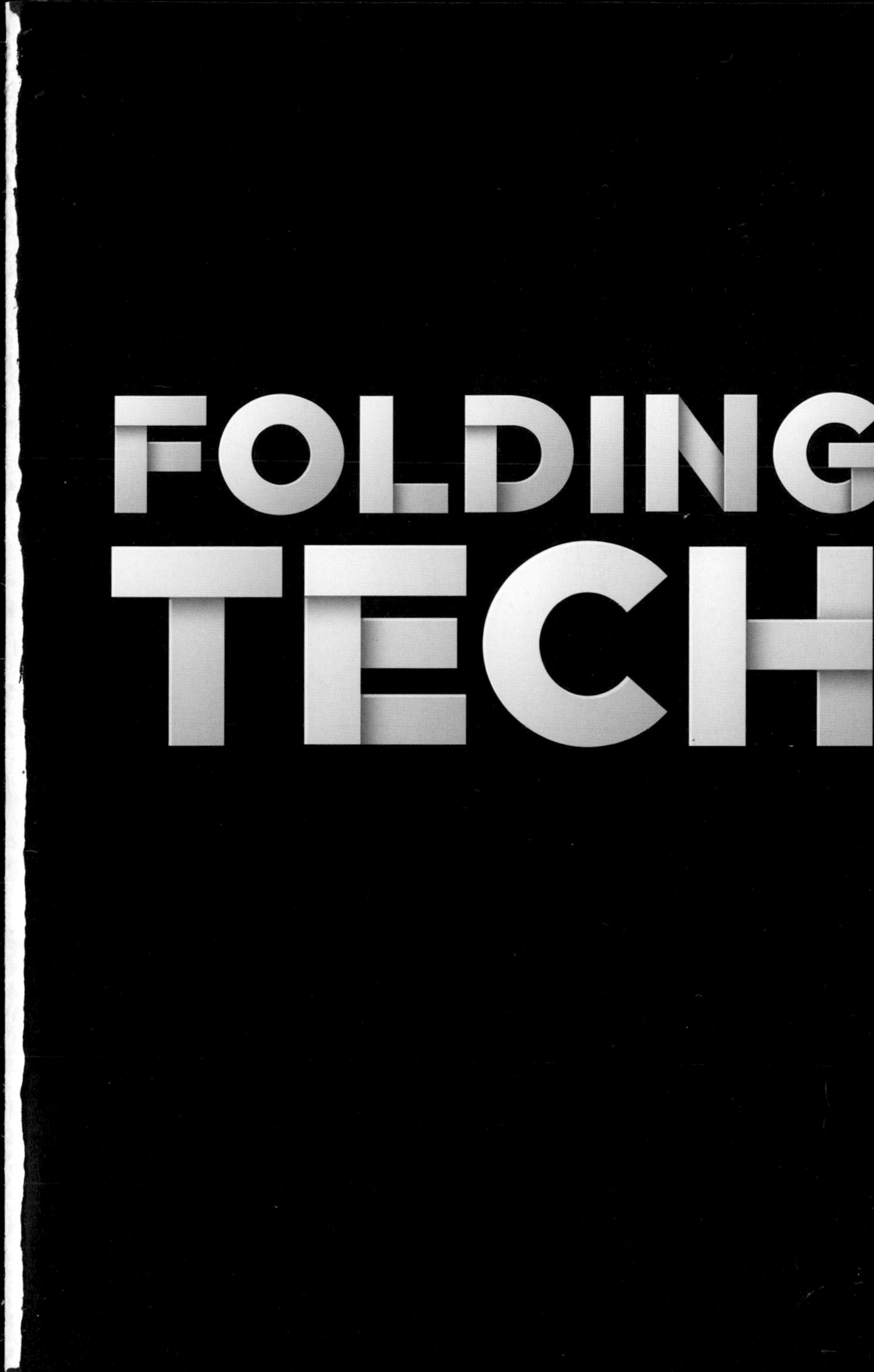
FOLDING
TECH

FOLDING TECH

USING ORIGAMI AND NATURE TO REVOLUTIONIZE TECHNOLOGY

KAREN LATCHANA KENNEY

TWENTY-FIRST CENTURY BOOKS / MINNEAPOLIS

To an extraordinary mathematician, Maximilian

Text copyright © 2021 by Lerner Publishing Group, Inc.

All rights reserved. International copyright secured. No part of this book may be reproduced, stored in a retrieval system, or transmitted in any form or by any means—electronic, mechanical, photocopying, recording, or otherwise—without the prior written permission of Lerner Publishing Group, Inc., except for the inclusion of brief quotations in an acknowledged review.

Twenty-First Century Books™
An imprint of Lerner Publishing Group, Inc.
241 First Avenue North
Minneapolis, MN 55401 USA

For reading levels and more information, look up this title at www.lernerbooks.com.

Main body text set in Adobe Garamond.
Typeface provided by Adobe.

Library of Congress Cataloging-in-Publication Data

Names: Kenney, Karen Latchana, author.
Title: Folding tech : using origami and nature to revolutionize technology / by Karen Latchana Kenney.
Description: Minneapolis, MN : Twenty-First Century Books, an imprint of Lerner Publishing Group, Inc., [2020] | Includes bibliographical references and index. | Audience: Age 12–18. | Audience: Grades 9–12.
Identifiers: LCCN 2019009069 | ISBN 9781541533042 (lb : alk. paper)
Subjects: LCSH: Origami—Industrial applications—Juvenile literature. | Biomimicry—Juvenile literature. | Machine design—Juvenile literature. | Folds (Form)—Juvenile literature.
Classification: LCC TT872.5 .K46 2020 | DDC 736/.982—dc23

LC record available at https://lccn.loc.gov/2019009069

Manufactured in the United States of America
1-44867-35723-5/5/2020

A special thanks
go to the following people for their insight, time,
and research on origami mathematics and technology:

Thomas Hull: a mathematics professor at Western New England University, Hull is an origami artist who creates modular designs and is a renowned expert on the mathematics of origami.

Robert J. Lang: a former physicist and engineer and now a full-time origami artist, Lang is an origami mathematics pioneer whose complex origami designs include realistic and detailed representations of the natural world.

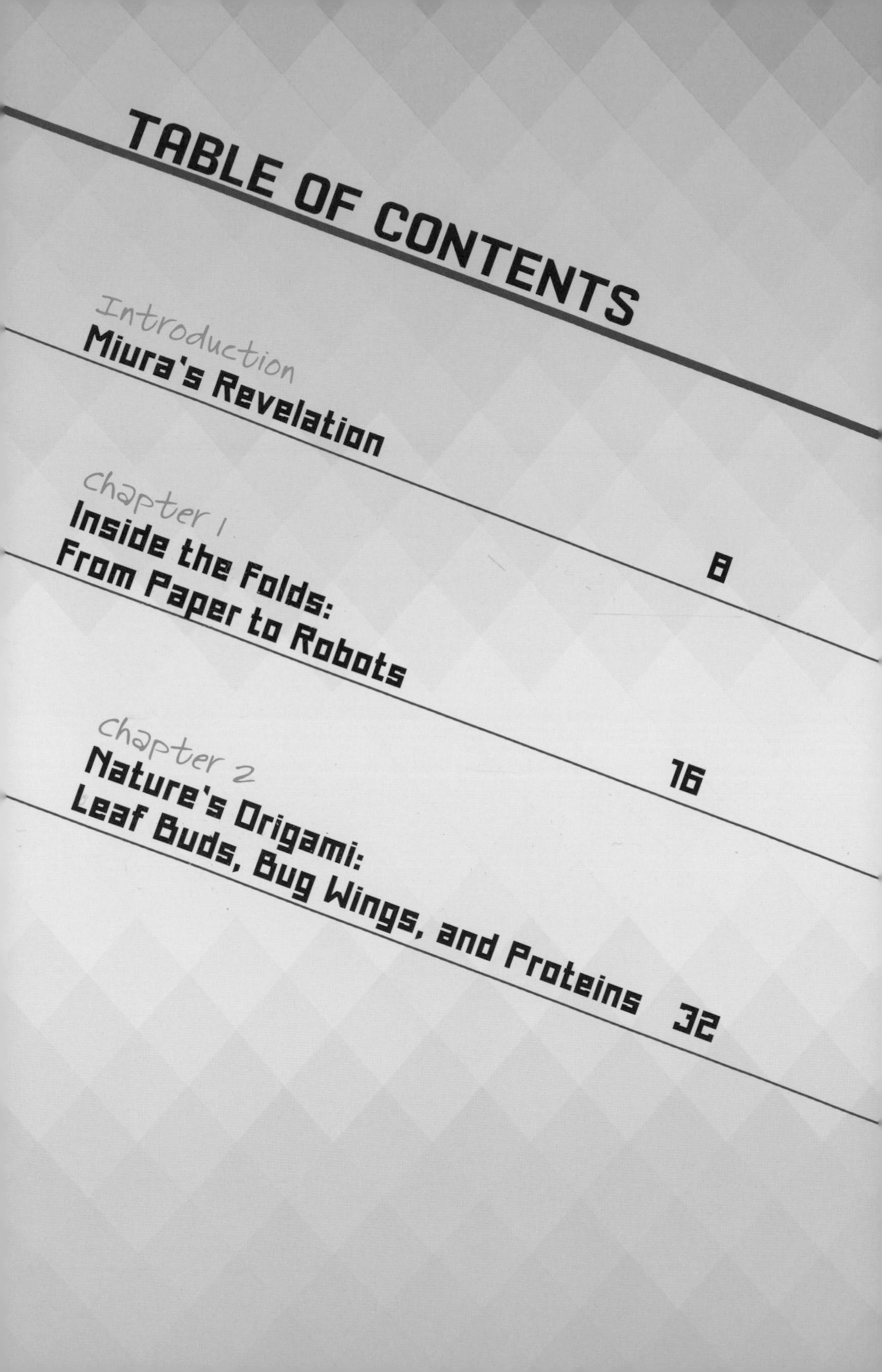

TABLE OF CONTENTS

INTRODUCTION
MIURA'S REVELATION

Smoke billows on a launchpad as the engines of a rocket start. The engines, fighting against gravity's tremendous pull, have to push the rocket's heavy payload roughly 60 miles (97 km) into the air to break through Earth's atmosphere and enter space. Inside that payload is the *Juno* space probe, which has been in development for years. Its equipment has been packed tightly inside the tip of the long, narrow rocket, which mostly consists of fuel for the engines. After several tense minutes, the rocket leaves Earth behind and enters the darkness of space. The rocket releases its payload, and the probe begins its journey. But first, it needs to generate power. It slowly unfurls its three winglike solar panels, which span 9 feet (2.7 m) across and 30 feet (9.1 m) long, and begins making electricity for its mission. By generating this power, the *Juno* probe can make its long journey to Jupiter.

Back on Earth, a swarm of tiny robots gathers at a tornado disaster site. Just minutes before, each robot was a flat piece with layers made of different materials. When exposed to heat, the layers transform and fold into new shapes as the robots automatically assemble themselves. Once they are finished, the robots begin their collective mission of photographing the wreckage and looking for survivors in areas too dangerous for humans to explore.

INCREDIBLE FOLDING TECH

These seemingly unrelated technologies have something very important in common. Their materials are strategically folded to fit large surfaces inside a small container or transform a flat object into a piece of technology that can move and perform tasks. Folding sounds simple—almost too simple—to be a solution to advanced engineering problems, yet it can be geometrically complex. With high mountain and deep valley creases, and points where both converge, folding creates amazingly compact, strong, and complicated structures.

The use of folding in technology is a recent development inspired by the ancient Japanese art of origami, in which artists change two-dimensional paper into three-dimensional objects. Origami starts simply—just a paper square with two sides, each a different color or pattern. The only tools you use are your hands and your imagination—no scissors, no glue, no tape. Nothing is added or taken away. Even within these limitations, folded paper can become almost anything. And it starts with that first fold, which changes the paper's shape completely. Now it's a triangle or rectangle. A second fold changes it again. Fold after fold brings new possibilities, and that simple paper square can take the shape of an elephant, a goldfish, or even a prickly cactus.

Folded paper creates beautiful artistic sculptures. But there's much more to folding than the art it can become. These folds are very interesting in technological design. They have the ability to turn

The James Webb Space Telescope, set to launch in 2021, will be the successor to the famous Hubble Space Telescope. Webb's mirror measures 21 feet (6.4 m) across, allowing it to see farther into space than the Hubble, whose mirror is only 7.9 feet (2.4 m) in diameter. Because of its size, the James Webb Space Telescope has to be folded up for launch and be able to unfold itself once in orbit.

something very large into something very small without losing any material at all. And if you look closely at these folds, you'll see that they are ruled by some pretty complex mathematics. As mathematicians have discovered, and continue to explore, folding follows predictable patterns. These patterns are not limited to origami art—they can be found throughout the natural world.

For example, look at a leaf bud. Tightly packed inside is a much larger leaf, folded perfectly, preparing to spread out and catch the sun's rays. Those rays are filled with energy that plants convert into food so they can grow and live. Solar panels also catch the sun's energy, converting it into electricity that powers machines. Both leaves and solar panels need a large surface area to capture as much sunlight as possible. Solar panels are an ideal power source for spacecraft, which have unlimited access to sunlight while in space. But getting them into space isn't easy. Solar panels need to travel into space inside long, thin rockets. And they need to easily expand to their full size once in space.

MAKING THE MIURA-ORI

How could you fit a solar array inside a rocket? And then how could it unfold once it was in space without an astronaut to help? Japanese astrophysicist Koryo Miura, one of the founders of origami engineering, considered these questions in his research. Miura had been interested in space structures and folding since his college days. In the 1970s, he studied an ancient folding pattern he believed could be used in technological design. This pattern has mountain and valley folds that make a tessellation (repeating pattern) of identical parallelograms skewed six to ten degrees off a right angle. Using this pattern, Miura could compress a large flat surface into the compact, flat shape of one repeated parallelogram. By pulling on the corners of the paper, he could then easily expand the folded piece back to its full size. And it was easy to compress again too.

Miura called his pattern the developable double corrugation surface, which wasn't a terribly catchy name. Luckily, the British Origami Society stepped in and gave it a more memorable one. They called it the Miura-ori, Japanese for Miura's Fold. The folding pattern was perfect for maps and newspapers (the official Tokyo subway map uses Miura's Fold), but Miura had something bigger in mind. He had created Miura's Fold specifically for use in space.

In 1985 he proposed using the Miura-ori with stiff, rigid materials for solar arrays. Since this kind of technology uses materials much thicker than paper, the "folds" are made with hinges that connect stiff, flat panels to make a solar array. The Miura-ori was the perfect solution

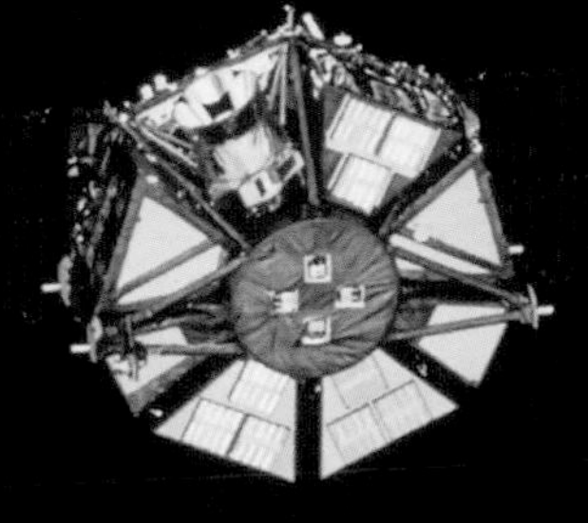

In addition to the Miura-ori experiment aboard the Space Flyer Unit, the spacecraft carried Japanese fire-bellied newt eggs to observe how gravity affects their hatching process.

for condensing a solar array into a flat and compact shape that could fit inside a rocket. Its opening and refolding could be easily done by machinery too.

Miura's Fold made its first expedition into space with the Japanese research vessel Space Flyer Unit, which launched on March 18, 1995, and contained a number of experiments, including the Miura-ori. The vessel's solar panels were folded up tightly using the Miura-ori pattern, one stacked atop the other. Packed inside a Japanese H-II rocket, the Space Flyer Unit launched into orbit. Then the Space Flyer Unit was released, and its experimental solar array was successfully deployed. Miura's Fold had worked!

With that first application in the Space Flyer Unit, origami and technology fused to bring technological design into a new era. Folding technology had entered space. Where else could it go?

MIURA-ORI: DIY

Anyone can make the Miura-ori. You just need a piece of paper and some patience. In about a half hour, you'll see the genius of this unique folding pattern.

You'll Need

- piece of 8.5-inch-by-11-inch (21.6 cm by 28 cm) paper or A3 paper (11.7 inches by 16.5 inches, or 29.7 cm by 42 cm)
- ruler
- pencil

Here's How

1. Fold the paper into five equal vertical sections. You will make four folds to do so. Fold like an accordion, so each fold switches between a mountain and valley fold.

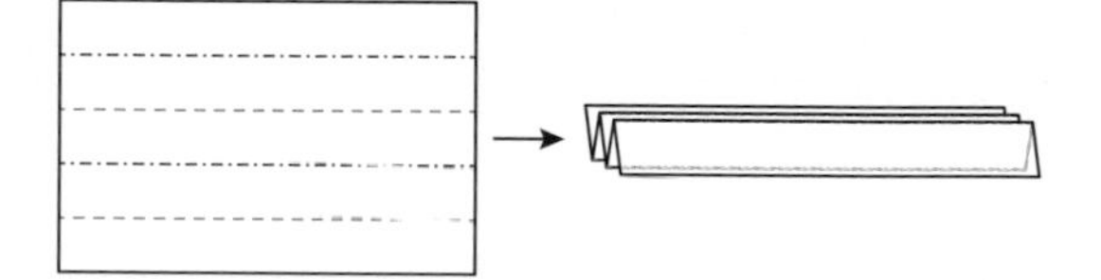

2. The paper is now a long, thin rectangle. Keep it folded this way as you continue folding the paper. Use the ruler to mark seven equal sections of the long rectangle.

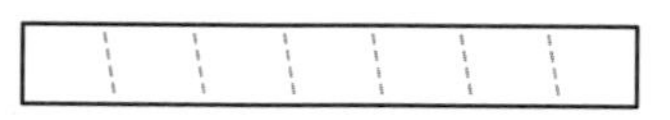

3. Make the first fold by bringing three sections up from the bottom. Fold at a slight angle to the left. Make it so the top left corner of the folded end is 1 inch (2.5 cm) from the top of the other end and 0.25 inch (0.6 cm) from the left edge of the unfolded end.

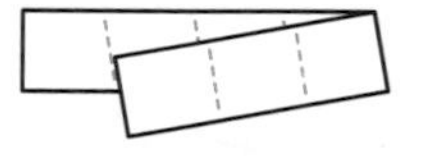

4. Fold that folded section back down. Make its right edge parallel with the right edge of the unfolded end.

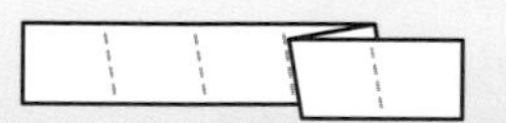

5. Keep folding the remaining two sections of the rectangle in this way. Then flip the rectangle over and continue folding the remaining four sections, keeping the angles parallel to one another. Make sure the folds are crisp and tight.

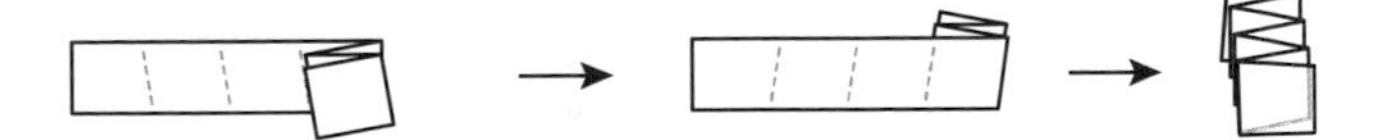

6. Unfold the paper so that it is flat. You'll see that the seven sections you just folded make seven zigzag lines. Start at the top zigzag line, and make it a mountain fold. Move the second zigzag line, and make it a valley fold. Continue alternating between mountain and valley folds for these seven zigzag lines.

7. Fold the paper up from left to right along the mountain and valley folds. Fold it down from the top to the bottom of the folded rectangle. At this point, the paper is compressed into the completed Miura's Fold. To open it up again, just pull on opposite corners of the paper, and it will quickly and easily unfold.

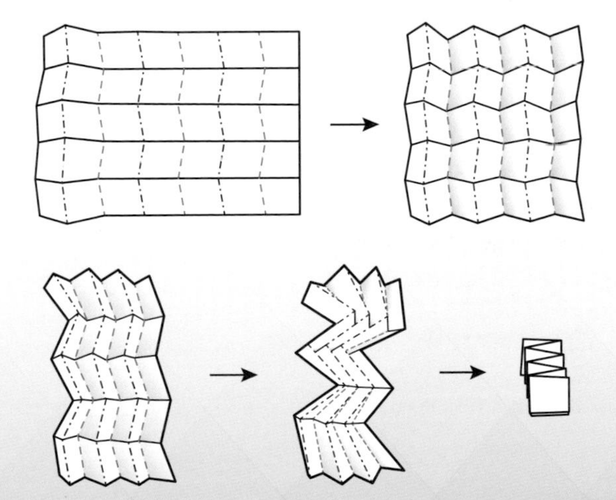

CHAPTER 1
INSIDE THE FOLDS:
From Paper to Robots

Folding technology didn't catch on right away in the science, mathematics, and engineering communities. After all, origami is an art form often linked with the paper cranes many people learn how to make as a kid. It was hard to take it seriously at first. But origami gradually became more popular as mathematicians, scientists, and engineers saw how its interesting patterns could create valuable technological designs. Folding and origami can solve physics problems that puzzle even the best engineers. In a surprising historical twist, something as ancient as the art of origami has evolved to inspire some of the most cutting-edge technological designs.

ORIGAMI'S ORIGINS

Origami has a long tradition in Japan, where artists and everyday people have practiced and refined its patterns for centuries. The name comes from the Japanese words for "fold" (*ori*) and "paper" (*gami*). Paper folding began in Japan in the seventh century, when paper was a valuable and rare material. This paper was made from plant and tree pulp flattened into molds and was first brought to the country by Chinese Buddhist monks. At first, people used paper folding only for religious ceremonial purposes. This early "origami" included the *shide* pattern, which uses both folding and cutting to make the zigzagging streamers that hang at Shinto shrines. Shinto is the national religion of Japan, and different forms of folded paper are significant within its shrines. Folded-paper ornaments called *noshi* were another early form. It became the custom to place a piece of dried seafood inside the *noshi* and attach it onto a wedding gift. These early forms of origami had no written instructions: people taught one another how to make them.

By the seventeenth century, paper folding had moved from the shrines to the public and became a form of recreation. With the development of a papermaking industry, paper could be mass-produced and was more easily available and cheaper to buy. Japanese people began regarding paper folding as an art form. It was no longer purely a sacred

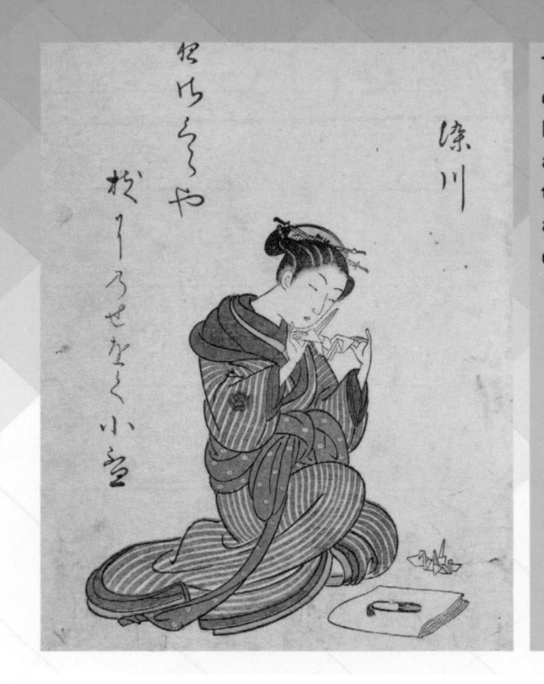

This 1770 painting shows a woman creating a paper-folding artwork. In front of her is a pair of scissors and sheets of paper. Paper folding that allows the use of scissors to assist in making the artworks is called *kirigami*.

practice. In 1797 the first very simple paper-folding instructions were published in the book *Orikata Tehon Chushingura* by publisher Yoshinoya Tamehachi of Kyoto, Japan. More people of all ages learned traditional folding patterns, including the crane, the water bomb, and different kinds of boxes. They practiced the traditional patterns they learned from their teachers or family and passed them on from one generation to the next. As a result, paper folding remained relatively the same, preserved in its traditional patterns, and few people outside of Japan knew about it.

Then, in the 1950s, origami master Akira Yoshizawa started gaining worldwide recognition for his uniquely exquisite and original origami designs. His work was exhibited in Europe and published in the Japanese magazine *Asahi Graph*. Soon the world knew of Yoshizawa *and* origami. His animal models of dogs, squirrels, wolves, horses, and more seemed imbued with life. He had mastered the basics of origami and then taken it to a new level. Known as the father of modern origami, Yoshizawa not only created new origami designs but also developed a system of dashed and dotted lines and arrows that

Sadako and Her Paper Cranes

Many kids around the world learn to make paper cranes, a symbol of peace and hope, as their very first piece of origami. It's an ancient Japanese pattern, but one little girl's story brought the paper crane to the world. Her name was Sadako Sasaki, and she was just two years old when she was exposed to radiation from the atomic bomb that the US dropped on Hiroshima, Japan, in 1945 before the end of World War II (1939–1945). The bomb destroyed her city and spread toxic radiation across the land and into people's bodies. Sadako was bathed in this radiation, which caused her to develop a form of cancer called leukemia nine years later.

A Japanese belief says that if you fold one thousand paper cranes, you can be granted a wish. Sadako wished to get well, and she began folding crane after crane while she was in the hospital being treated for leukemia. Her brother believed she put her pain into every crane, never letting others know how much she was hurting inside. When Sadako died in 1955, her classmates started a campaign to build a monument in Sadako's memory. In 1958 a statue of Sadako holding a golden crane was erected in the Hiroshima Peace Memorial Park. Her story spread around the world through Austrian author Robert Jungk's book *Children of the Ashes*. Western efforts to ban atomic bombs used Sadako as a symbol for their movement. Sadako and her paper cranes grew to symbolize the hope for a more peaceful world. While learning about her story, nuclear bombs, and peace movements in school, children often learn how to fold origami paper cranes too.

Many people send their paper cranes to Hiroshima, and the city puts them by Sadako's statue. Close to ten million cranes arrive each year from all over the world. Sadako's family has also sent her cranes to places in need of peace and healing. The first were sent to the National 9/11 Memorial & Museum, which commemorates the September 11, 2001, attacks on the World Trade Center in New York City. In 2011, when an earthquake triggered a tsunami that hit Japan and caused a meltdown at a nuclear power plant, the September 11th Families' Association and the 9/11 Tribute Center sent a gift to Japan: a welded metal origami crane made from the debris of the World Trade Center.

Akira Yoshizawa poses with some of his creations.

communicated the instructions for his designs. He first published these instructions in his 1954 book *Atarashii Origami Geijutsu*. This system allowed anyone to create origami. They did not need to be able to read Japanese. Western origami authors adopted Yoshizawa's language in their own books, and it became the standard way to show others how to make a piece of origami. Because of Yoshizawa's international fame and his easy-to-understand system of instructions, origami has spread throughout the world, inspiring new generations of modern origamists.

MODERN ORIGAMI

With Yoshizawa's and other artists' new interpretations of this ancient art, origami sculptures broke free from being the traditional flat interpretations of shapes seen in nature. Modern origami could take on round shapes and seem more lifelike. A carp fish could have scales and whiskers, just like a real one. A beetle could have tiny pincers at the tips of each leg. Realistic details like these were now possible because of the work of modern origamists, who studied the mathematical

The Universal Language of Origami

Origami is made from a combination of mountain and valley folds. Here's the system Yoshizawa created, which was later adopted and changed slightly by Western origami authors Samuel L. Randlett and Robert Harbin. The system uses dashed and dotted lines and arrows. With a series of diagrams using these symbols, a reader can learn how to make an origami sculpture. A fold pattern shows a complete guideline for making origami in one diagram.

Origami consists of two kinds of folds:

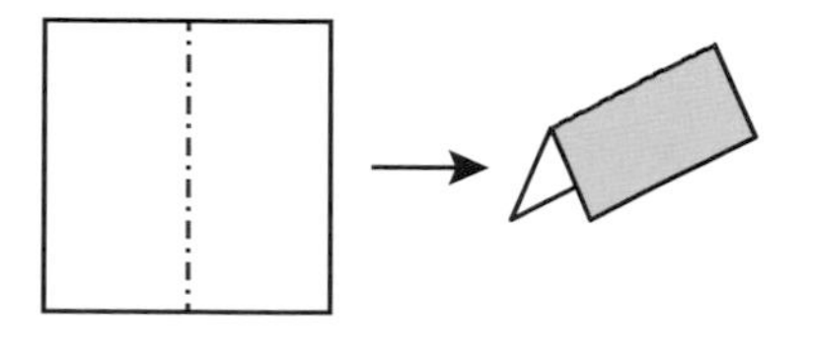

mountain fold

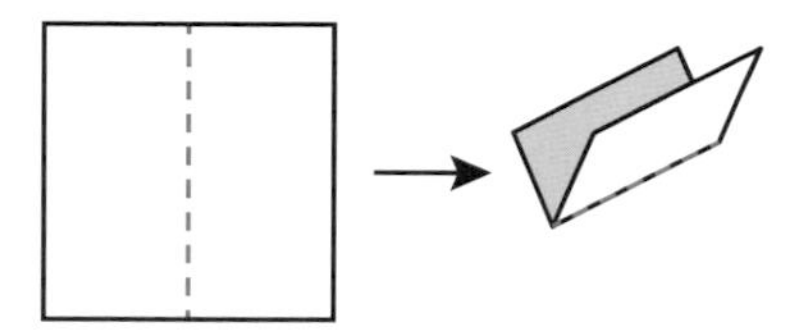

These are the five kinds of lines shown on an origami diagram:

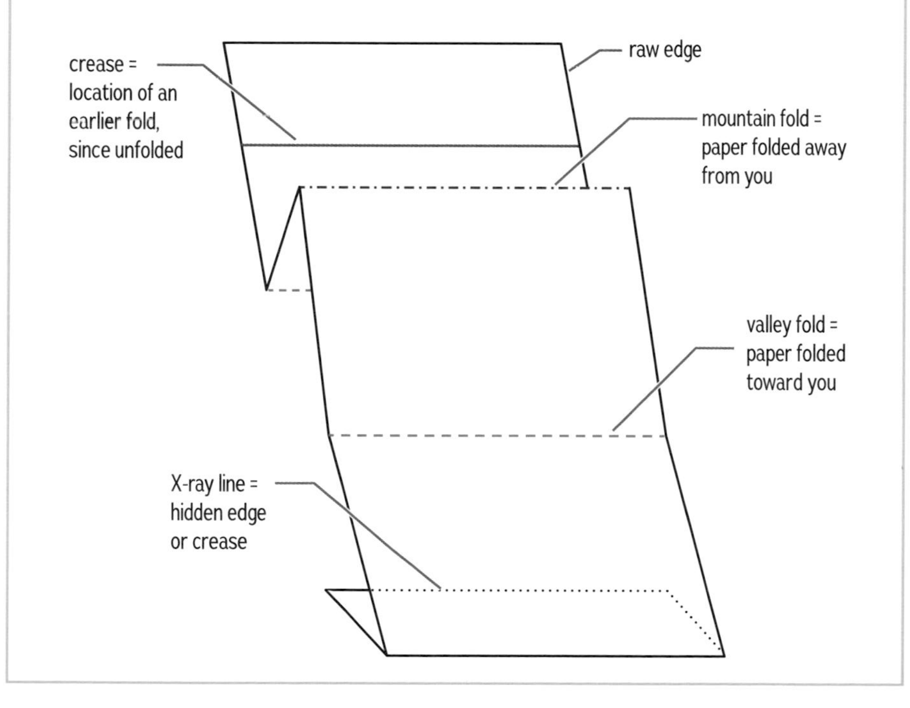

and geometrical patterns in origami's folds. Unfold an origami piece to reveal its geometry in the lines that make its folds. Within this blueprint for the finished piece are triangles, quadrangles, vertices, acute and obtuse angles, and more. Those shapes and angles follow rules to successfully create an origami piece. Studying what those rules are and how they work has led to new discoveries of what folding can create. Modern origamists are finding that almost any 3D shape imaginable can be made from paper with origami. It just takes some new tools and ways of thinking about folding.

Miura made his folding discovery in the 1970s and proved origami could be a practical solution to engineering problems, such as getting a solar array into space and then extending it to capture sunlight, in addition to being a beautiful art form. But Miura was not alone in studying how origami could be used in science and engineering—many people around the world were studying the complexities of origami and its folds. In 1989 scientists, mathematicians, and origamists gathered in Ferrara, Italy, for an international scientific conference to share the ways origami, mathematics, and science intersected. This sharing of knowledge helped to rapidly advance origami science and mathematics, and the conferences became known as the Origami in Science, Mathematics, and Education (OSME) conferences. Since 1989 there have been seven OSME conferences around the world, and many of their proceedings are printed in book form. Attendees share mathematical models of origami and different applications and research into origami science—from computer tools that create origami designs to how much energy folded materials could absorb from a car crash.

One of those early origami science pioneers is former NASA engineer, physicist, and origamist Robert J. Lang. He makes some of the most complex origami sculptures in the world and is a leader in the field of computational origami, a branch of computer science that studies algorithms to solve paper-folding problems. In the early 1990s, he created a computer program called TreeMaker for designing complex origami patterns. The program turns a line drawing of a shape or figure, such as a tree or an animal, into an origami folding pattern. Each line in the drawing represents an appendage in the final sculpture: an arm or a leg, an antenna, or a jaw. It does so using a technique called circle-river packing. The program changes the stick figure into geometric shapes—circles and rivers, which assign areas of paper to be folded. Each circle in the design represents the minimum amount of paper needed to create a folded appendage. The longer the appendage, the bigger the circle. Each river in the design makes folded sections that connect appendages—such as the body segments of an insect—and the longer the section, the wider the river.

Using mathematics, his computer programs, and his skill and imagination, Lang has created origami sculptures in the shapes of a cuckoo clock, a hummingbird feeding from a trumpet blossom, a sea urchin, and many more intricate designs. He names his pieces in the

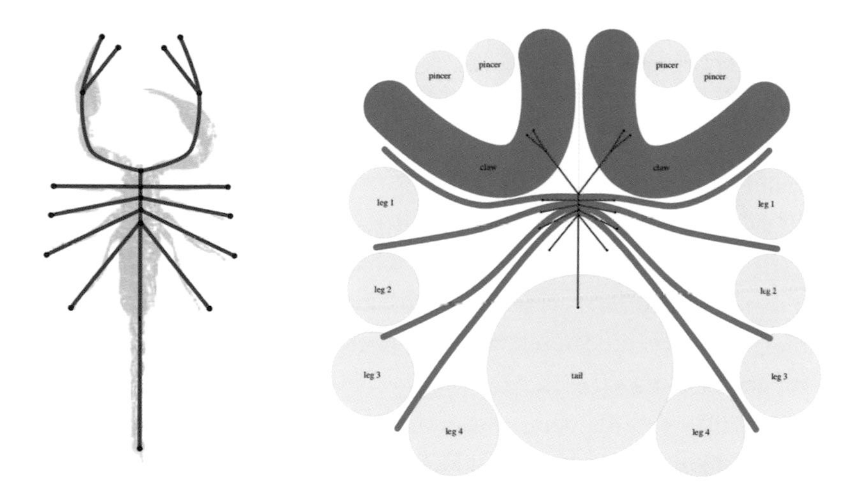

This illustration by Lang demonstrates the circle-river packing method for an origami scorpion design. His TreeMaker program transforms a stick figure (*left*) into the figure made of circles and "rivers" (*right*).

style of orchestral compositions, such as *Perching Cardinal, Opus 689* for an origami red cardinal perching on a branch. He uses this naming style because he believes origami is similar to music in that there are two distinct artistic forms: the "composition" (or design) and then its expression or performance (in origami, the actual fold).

"From a single composition, I and other artists can 'perform' (or fold) that composition as individual artistic expressions, each with its own character and distinct treatment," Lang explained. "I serially number my compositions (giving them a number when I've made sufficient notes that I could re-create the work from my notes), and use 'Opus' in the same way that musicians do, as an identifier of the composition."

Lang's compositions have been displayed in art museums and other exhibitions around the world, from the Museum of Modern Art in New York City to the Badisches Landesmuseum in Karlsruhe, Germany. He's known for his incredible artistic creations, but he's also known for his work with technological design. Engineering companies and research laboratories hire Lang to consult with them on projects involving folding. Lang can't talk about many of the high-tech projects he's involved with, because he signed a contract preventing him from discussing them.

But among the more public projects Lang has worked on is the Eyeglass lens, a space telescope lens he helped design in 2000. Working with the Lawrence Livermore National Laboratory, Lang developed a folding pattern for a telescope lens that could fit inside a rocket with a diameter of just 13 feet (4 m). Once unfolded, the lens would be 328 feet (100 m) in diameter, about the size of a football field, on a telescope as long as Manhattan. Using an umbrella-shaped origami pattern, the laboratory created and tested a prototype of the Eyeglass lens that was 16.4 feet (5 m) across when unfolded and 5 feet (1.5 m) when folded. The prototype both folded and unfolded perfectly.

Lang has also worked with German engineering company EASi,

which consulted him when they wanted an algorithmic description of how to fold car airbags into a dashboard. Airbags usually sit compactly within a car's body around the seats. When there's a crash, the airbags rapidly inflate with a gas and break through the car's body to act as cushions for the passengers. Different airbags have different shapes. Spherical, oblong, and doughnut-shaped airbags cushion in different ways. Airbag designers wanted to use computer simulations to figure out which folding patterns would work best for each shape. So the company approached Lang. He had a computer algorithm for insect origami patterns that he thought would work for their airbag simulation program. They incorporated his algorithm into their program, and the simulation worked.

TWENTY-FIRST CENTURY ORIGAMI ENGINEERING

Through the early work of Miura, Lang, and many other modern origamists, the use of origami in science and technology gained momentum. What makes folding especially important in engineering is its ability to bend, stretch, and curve materials in ways that, at first glance, seem impossible, allowing large objects to fit into small spaces or transforming flat sheets into 3D shapes.

In 2012 and 2013, origami engineering got a big boost. The National Science Foundation, a federal agency that funds scientific research, awarded thirteen grants for research projects that focused on what the foundation called Origami Design for Integration of Self-assembling Systems for Engineering Innovation (ODISSEI). Each of these ODISSEI grants gave close to $2 million to cutting-edge research projects at universities and science facilities around the United States. The funded projects included origami with non-paper materials, light-activated folding, programmable folding, and folding so small that it's at a microscale.

One group of recipients came from the Massachusetts Institute of Technology (MIT). It included Professors Erik Demaine and Daniela Rus.

Simple Rules, Enormous Possibilities: Robert J. Lang

When he was six years old, Robert J. Lang began what would become his lifelong relationship with origami. Working from a book, he learned to fold some simple shapes from the scrap paper lying around in his home. "And I could fold all these wonderful different patterns," Lang says. "Then, that got me interested, and I wanted to learn how to fold more and more different and diverse patterns." Eventually, Lang wanted to fold shapes of various animals but couldn't find the patterns to make the ones he wanted. So around the age of ten, he began creating his own patterns. His first design was a boat, and many more designs followed.

Lang became hooked on origami. Its limitations were especially intriguing. "It's a combination of the simplicity of the concept: a sheet of material and folding, and that's all," he says. "And folding is a pretty restrictive set of rules because you can't add material or take material away. But in origami, the sheet you start with is the sheet you end with. So you have this very tightly restricted set of rules, and yet there seems to be no end to the beauty, to the range of subjects we can create, to the artistic expression."

As Lang grew older, he continued folding, but it wasn't until his college classes at the California Institute of Technology that he became interested in the mathematics behind origami's folds. He realized that he could use mathematical ideas to create origami designs. What he was surprised to learn was that "the math itself of origami was also quite beautiful." Lang began his journey of exploring origami art and its mathematical aspects simultaneously, and he found that "there's this continual flow of information and inspiration between the art and the math as I learn new mathematical concepts. Those [concepts] find a home in some of the art that I'm creating or, in some cases, some of the technological things I'm trying to develop using folding. And, conversely, art and technology raise new mathematical questions to be answered, and then I can go off and explore them and try to answer them."

After getting bachelor's and master's degrees in electrical engineering, Lang went on to get his PhD in applied physics. He worked for NASA in the Jet Propulsion Laboratory (JPL) for four and a half years and then at SDL, a company in Silicon Valley, doing laser research and development for nine years. He left SDL in 2001 to become a full-time origami artist, author, and consultant. He creates origami art for collectors and advertising, teaches and lectures about origami, gives workshops on using folding in design, and

Lang folding a new piece of origami using a large piece of paper

consults with laboratories and companies on the applications of folding to solve technological problems.

After fifty years of folding, Lang is now known worldwide as being one of the masters of origami. He has been in several documentaries about origami, including two that were shown on PBS: *Between the Folds* and *NOVA*'s *The Origami Revolution*. He's given a TED talk on the math and artistry of origami and written many books about origami and mathematics, including *Twists, Tilings, and Tessellations: Mathematical Methods for Geometric Origami*. As Lang has become a master folder over the years, his designs have become more complex. One of his most complicated is of a cactus with many prickly spines. It took Lang close to seven years, off and on, to fold this masterpiece, which he calls *Cactus, Opus 680*. Origami is a way of life for Lang, and he couldn't imagine it not being so. As he continues to create his origami designs and compositions, Lang says, "The more I explore origami, the more potential I find, the more creating new expressions of art."

A self-folding robot transitions from one shape to another as it prepares to walk.

They had been working for a few years to develop a simple robot that could change its shape by folding itself on command. Along with a team of researchers at Harvard University, their work resulted in a 3D-printable robot made of five layers of materials. The middle layer is copper etched into lines that conduct electricity. This is sandwiched between two layers of paper that give the robot structure. Then two motors attach to the top of the robot. Finally, the copper and paper layers are sandwiched between a polymer that shrinks when it gets hot, just as a Shrinky Dink does. The flat robot is put through a laser-cutting machine that creates the folding patterns. When the polymer heats up and shrinks along the lines drawn by the laser, the robot folds itself into a shape with four legs, each pair controlled by a motor. It can then walk away on its own. Demaine, Rus, and their team hope to make even bigger versions of these kinds of flat-packed self-folding robots and deploy them in harsh environments, such as on the surface of Mars or on a battlefield—places where people could be hurt or killed but where a robot would fare just fine.

Origami has led to many exciting technological possibilities, including these self-folding robots, and will lead to many more. The ODISSEI grant helped bring origami engineering into the technological mainstream. Many scientists and engineers are beginning to discover how folding can help solve the problems of sending large technology into outer space and tiny technology into human bodies, as well as many frontiers in between.

ORIGAMI CRANE: DIY

Follow the instructions below to fold your own origami crane. Refer to the folding notation described on page 21 if you need help determining what type of fold each step requires you to make.

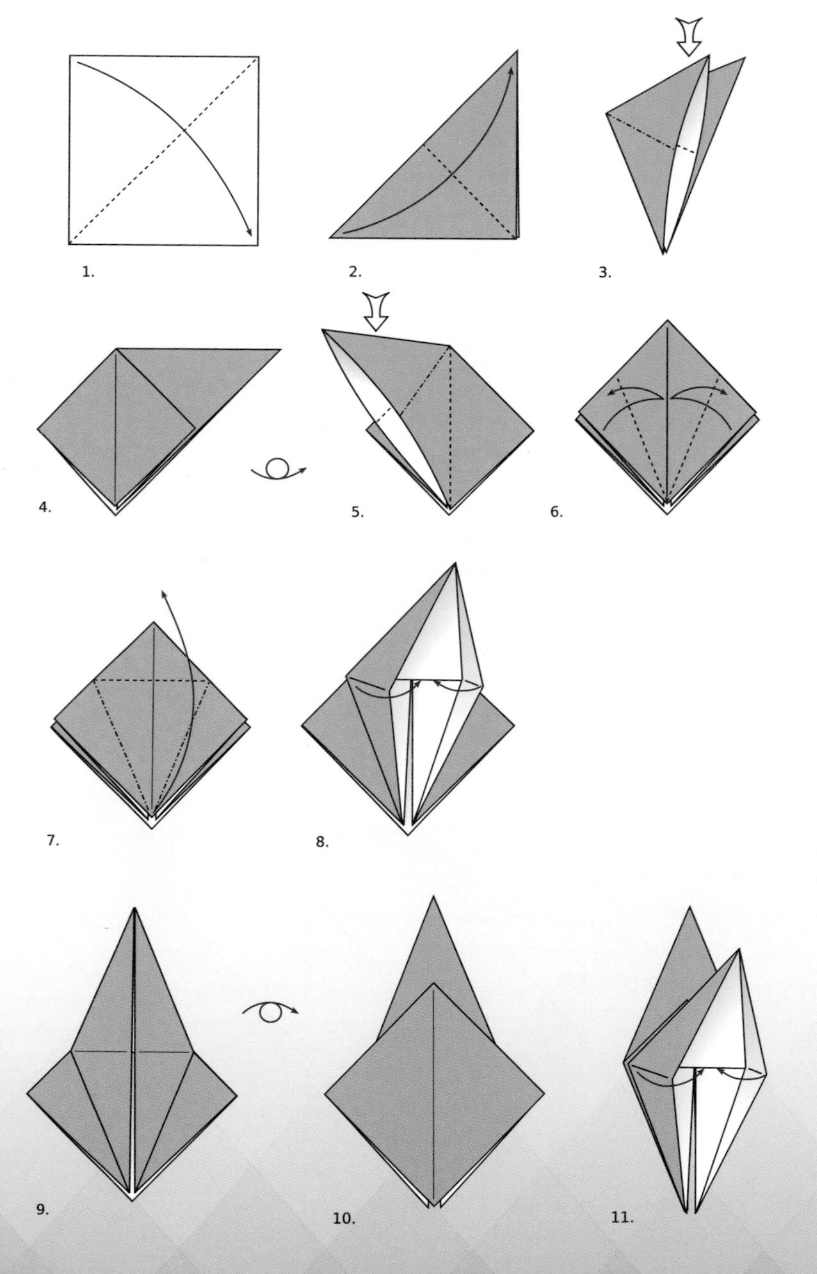

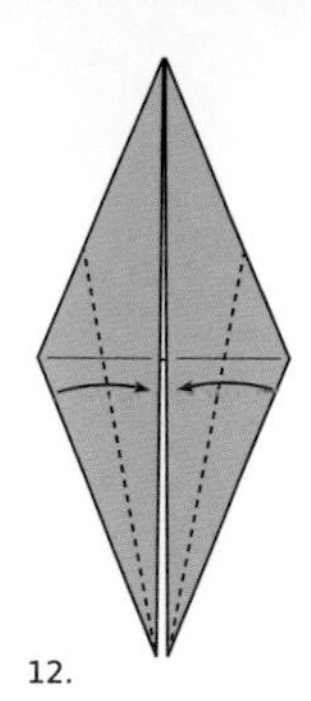

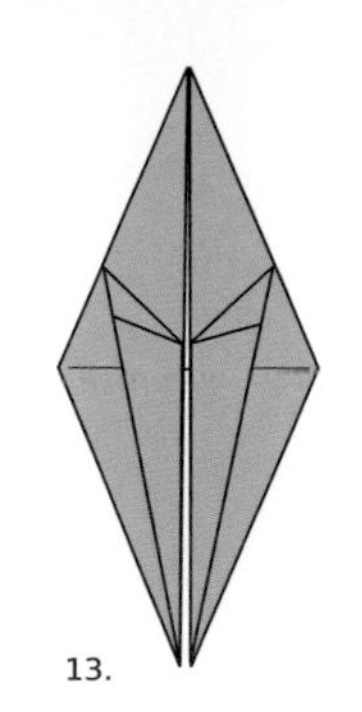

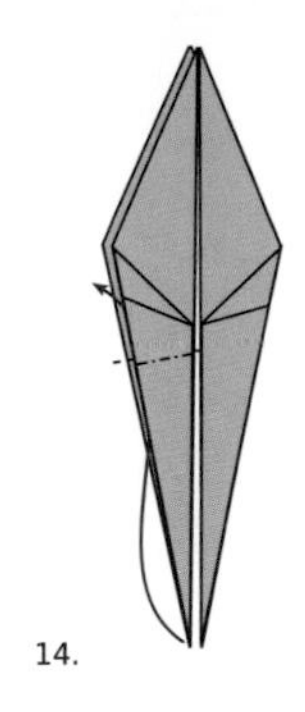

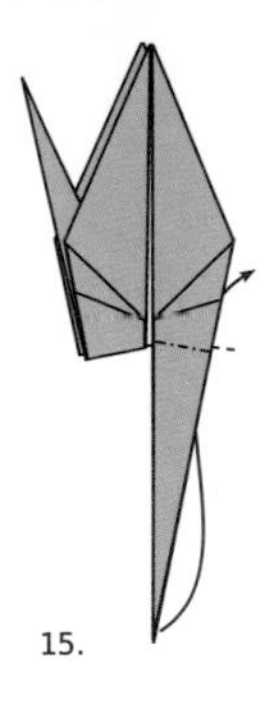

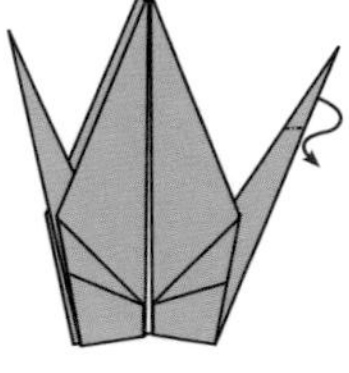

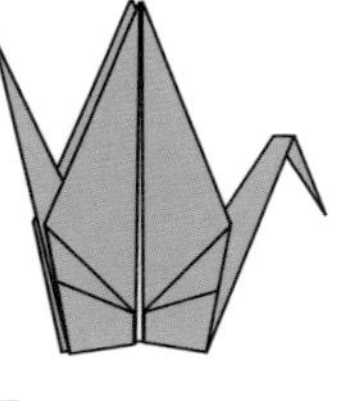

If you were to unfold your finished origami crane, you would see the crease pattern below:

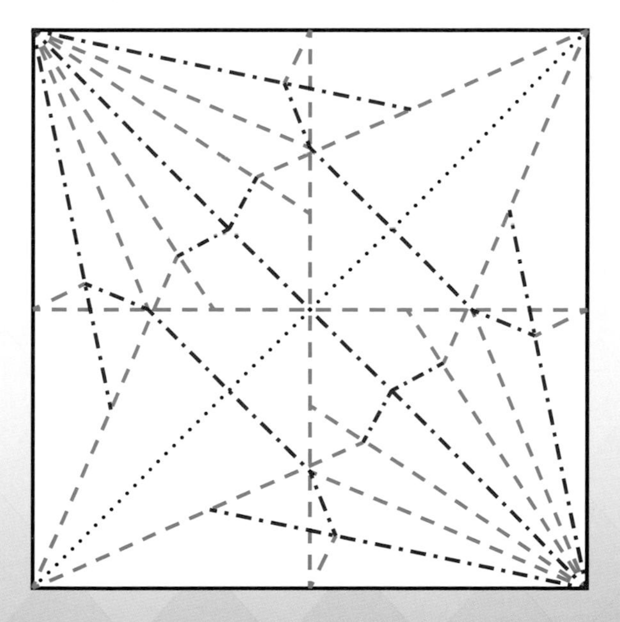

CHAPTER 2
NATURE'S ORIGAMI:
Leaf Buds, Bug Wings, and Proteins

Studying origami's geometry has also led scientists to notice and study folds in previously overlooked places—leaf buds, beetle wings, and even inside the human body. Long before origami became an art form, nature was folding too.

Nature began unfolding right before Biruta Kresling's eyes after meeting Korya Miura in 1989. The providential meeting happened at a conference in Budapest, Hungary, where Miura explained his Miura-ori to her. Kresling was intrigued and took that knowledge back with her to her teaching position in Valenciennes, a city in northern France. As an architect, design instructor, and researcher, Kresling was especially fascinated by folding structures and was looking for new ways to interest her design students in folding techniques. So she kept her eyes open and one day saw something remarkable on her walk to the school where she taught. Along the street were hornbeam trees—ordinary trees that she had passed by daily but never really noticed before—filled with stiffly pleated teardrop-shaped leaves. This day Kresling looked closely at the leaves, and she noticed something very unusual about them—they had a corrugated pattern. It was very similar to the Miura-ori. Kresling wanted to know more about these seemingly ordinary leaves and decided to study the leaves closely to figure out how their corrugations folded.

Kresling modeled the leaves' pattern with origami using a simple form of the Miura-ori. She worked out the leaf pattern: It had a central vein running from its petiole (where the leaf attaches to the stem) to its tip. On both sides of the central vein were parallel-angled mountain and valley folds that created a corrugated surface. When folded up, the leaf pattern was long and thin. Working out this leaf pattern helped explain how the hornbeam tree's leaves develop inside the bud. They grow in this tightly folded shape inside a compact bud covered in small scales. In springtime several long, thinly folded leaves emerge from each bud. Then they slowly open and unfold along the sides of the main vein until the leaves reach their full width.

Bioinspired Tech

Nature's been working out its problems for billions of years. Creatures and plants have evolved over time, retaining the features and behaviors that helped them survive in their environments. As different species developed, organisms varied slightly within each generation. As a simplified example, a population of mice may contain some individuals that run faster than others. The fastest mice survive longer because they can escape predators more easily. The longer they survive, the more babies they can have and, if genetics help determine running speed, the more likely their offspring will also be fast runners. This next generation of mice would contain more mice that are faster runners. This process of passing on the best traits for survival is how plants evolved to have large leaves folded up inside buds—so they could quickly unfold to capture sunlight and begin making food for the plant. And it's also how earwig wings became folded under protective hard elytra—it worked best for the insects that rarely fly and live in a mostly underground home.

These natural solutions are inspiring to scientists who often look to nature to help solve technological problems. Here are a few of the bioinspired technologies that scientists and engineers have designed:

- **Velcro.** The strips that hold everything from shoes to pens and equipment on spacecraft—hook-and-loop binding called Velcro—were inspired by burrs. In the 1940s, Swiss engineer George de Mestral noticed burrs stuck to his clothes after a hike. Burrs are seedpods that stick to animals' fur. Animals carry the seedpods with them to different places, where they fall off and begin growing into plants. Looking at the burrs under a microscope, de Mestral saw tiny hooks covering them. This led him to invent Velcro, which is made of two strips of fabric. One side is covered in hooks, and the other is covered in loops. When the strips touch, the hooks latch onto the loops, closing the strips together tightly, just like a zipper.
- **Self-cleaning paint.** Inspired by the leaves of lotus plants, this paint is used on building exteriors. The paint mimics the surface of a lotus leaf, which is covered in microscopic bumps. Water sits on top of the bumps, with a cushion of air between the water and the leaf's surface. Water does not stick to its surface; instead, it rolls off, taking dirt with it. All leaves have bumps like these, but the lotus is well known for being especially water repellent. Researchers used nanoparticles to create

the bumps in the paint, making peaks so small that they cannot be seen with the naked eye.

- **Superstrong tape.** Geckos are small lizards that can climb on any surface—even glass—and can hang upside down just by using their feet. That's because the toes on their feet are covered in tiny bristles. A gecko has close to five hundred thousand bristles on each foot. And each of those bristles is split into tinier bristles at their ends, resulting in a ton of microscopic bristles. When all these bristles touch a surface, a force of attraction called van der Waals forces arise. This force only occurs with tiny objects, but multiplied by many bristles over the whole area of a gecko's foot, the force can hold the gecko to seemingly smooth surfaces such as glass. The gecko's feet have inspired engineers to create strong adhesives that work in the same way. The adhesives have tiny hairs that poke up from the surface, making them a sticky but reusable adhesive. Engineers at Stanford University tested this kind of adhesive on pads for their hands connected to holders for their feet. Using the pads, engineer Elliot Hawkes climbed almost 12 feet (3.6 m) up a glass wall! The same team is working with NASA to create robots with gecko-inspired adhesive patches to catch space junk, such as old satellites that no longer work but continue to orbit Earth.

Gecko feet are very sticky, but the forces are unevenly distributed across their toes, so they can only lift up to a few pounds of weight. The Stanford University team's invention more evenly distributes force across the adhesive surface.

Kresling teamed up with biomimetics researchers Julian Vincent and Hidetoshi Kobayashi at the University of Reading to study the leaves' folding properties. Biomimetics is the study of the mechanics and materials found in nature. Biomimetics can be used in medicine, engineering, and technology to help solve human problems by mimicking nature's solutions. In 1998 Kresling's research team presented their findings to the British Royal Society. They analyzed the leaves mathematically and figured out the geometry within their folds. They found the angles of the folds and saw that leaves with larger angles could fold up more tightly. The researchers also worked out how much energy it took to unfold the leaves.

Her team's findings have important implications in engineering. Leaves are flexible and strong structures that can stand up to both wind and rain, and they can unfold in two directions at the same time—along the ribs and the central vein. Kresling's research has inspired engineers who design deployable structures, such as Miura's solar panels. The basic leaf pattern observed by Kresling can be arranged side by side in different combinations that could be used in different ways. Engineers are experimenting with these leaf-inspired folding patterns, which may someday be the basis for designs of folding roofs, tents, and antennas. It could even be used to deploy a kind of color-changing camouflage. Using a mechanism inspired by folding leaves, the camouflage could quickly unfold from a vehicle to disguise military troops, protecting them from harm during a battle.

HIDDEN WINGS

Leaf buds hide very simple but effective folds found in nature. But to find some of the most complicated folds in nature, check out the backs of certain bugs, where, hidden under hard, shell-like covers called elytra, large, delicate wings are tightly folded.

The earwig's elytra hide some of the most elaborately folded wings yet discovered. This small insect spends most of its time underground,

The team at ETH Zürich created a prototype earwig wing (*left*) that reproduced the folding and locking abilities of an earwig's natural wing (*right*).

where it has no need to fly. The hard elytra act as shields that protect its wings. When an earwig does need to take off, though, its lacy wings unfurl to become ten times larger than their folded shape. And it barely moves a muscle to do so. Traditional origami techniques could never produce an object that folded in the way the earwig's wings do. They seem to bypass the mathematical laws of origami. So what's the earwig's secret?

Researchers found the answer inside the wings' folds, or joints: they don't just fold—they also act like springs. These joints are made of resilin, a rubbery and stretchy kind of protein. Different thicknesses and positions of resilin in the joints provide different kinds of spring action in the wings, allowing them to stretch or twist. A locking joint at the central midpoint of the wings keeps the wings either open or closed. When locked, the joints store energy for the wings to use to move when unlocked. This is important because it means the insect does not need to use muscle energy to keep its wings stable or make them move, leaving the small insect with more energy to mate or to find food.

To discover these secrets, researchers André Studart and Jakob A. Faber from the university ETH Zürich in Switzerland, along with Andres Arrieta from Purdue University in Indiana, created a computer simulation of an earwig's wing. They then used their findings to design an object that worked in the same way as the wing. Using a 3D printer, they printed four plastic plates connected by a stretchy joint that imitated the earwig's wing movement. The plates unfolded, locked open, and then refolded with just the lightest touch. The researchers then used the same model to create the prototype for a folding, gripping object. It can self-fold, lock itself into place, and then grip objects without any added energy and in less than a second. "This means that we could get a robot gripper to lift something and hold it without any extra energy, or enable the robot to conform to the shape of whatever it's interacting with while still being able to hold that object," Arrieta said. Current robotic grippers have nowhere near the dexterity of human hands and have many issues gripping irregularly shaped objects. Being able to conform to an object's shape would make robotic grippers much more useful for many kinds of tasks.

Studart, Faber, and Arrieta believe this kind of self-locking folding

The earwig's wing inspired this folding gripper that is capable of grabbing and lifting objects without the use of electronics.

system modeled after the earwig wing could be used in space for solar sails, a large flat material that uses light to propel spacecraft. Without the need for an energy system to make it work, the sail would save space and weight—two valuable commodities inside a small rocket that needs to be light enough to break through Earth's gravity. This folding system could also be used for pop-up compact and super lightweight tents, foldable electronics, and packaging. "Once you've unfolded these things, it's often impossible to fold them back to their original shape. If, on the other hand, they simply refolded automatically, this would save a lot of hassle," said Faber.

LEARNING FROM LADYBUGS

Like earwigs, beetles have delicately folded wings. One common beetle in the United States is the round little ladybug. Underneath its spotted elytra are wings that can unfold to a length four times that of the ladybug's body. When ready to take off, ladybugs lift their elytra. Then their see-through wings laced with veins unfold in less than a tenth of a second. Ladybugs move their wings up, down, backward, and forward as they fly through the air. After they land, the ladybugs close their elytra and refold their wings underneath in about two seconds. Scientists weren't sure how the wings folded up, since their folds are hidden under the beetle's elytra. But an ingenious study done by Japanese researchers at the University of Tokyo in 2017 has revealed what's going on under the ladybug's shields.

They studied the ladybug because, "compared with other beetles, ladybugs are very good at flying and frequently take off," said Assistant Professor Kazuya Saito, one of the study's authors and a foldable-structure designer. "I thought their wing transformation systems are excellent and have [a] large potential for engineering." Saito's main research focus is solar array and antenna reflector design, and he thought researching the beetles would provide new ways to fold these technologies for use in space.

A ladybug in the process of unfolding its wings

When the researchers started their study, they weren't sure how they'd be able to capture the folding process. They tried taking high-speed pictures of a ladybug retracting its wings, but that didn't reveal how they folded. They needed to see the wing-folding process as it happened under the elytra, but the elytra blocked their view. They tried 3D printing an artificial ladybug elytron to put on the beetle, but they couldn't make one that was transparent. What worked was an idea proposed by the researchers' secretary—using clear UV-cured resin, a material often used in nail art, to make the artificial elytron. The researchers made the tiny elytron by hand, putting the resin in a silicon mold. Then they removed two-thirds of the right-side elytron on a living ladybug and transplanted the resin piece onto the remaining one-third. This created a transparent elytron that functioned as a window to the folded wing below.

How to Fold like a Ladybug

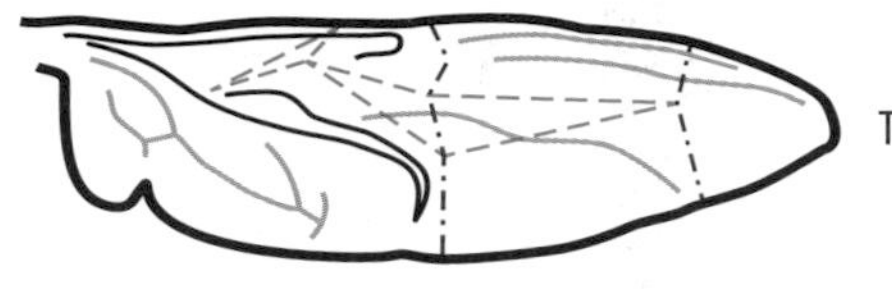

The crease pattern of the wing's folds

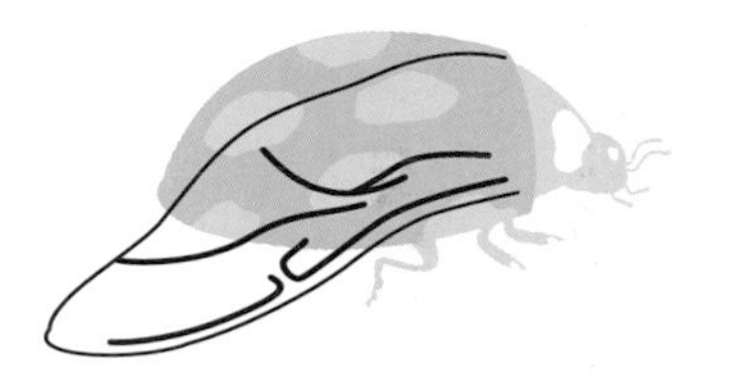

1. The elytron closes over the wing.

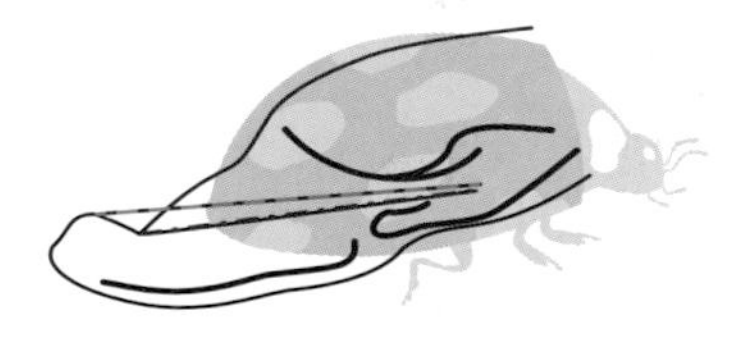

2. The elytron holds the wing in place, and it folds slightly in one direction. A triangular crease pattern emerges on the wing.

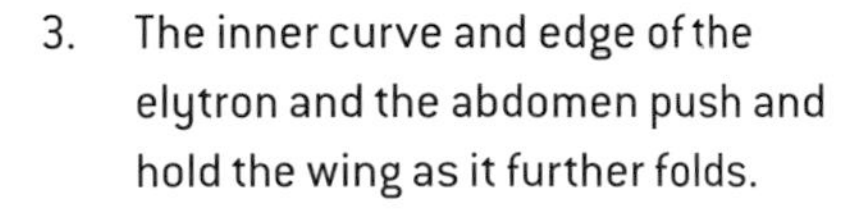

3. The inner curve and edge of the elytron and the abdomen push and hold the wing as it further folds.

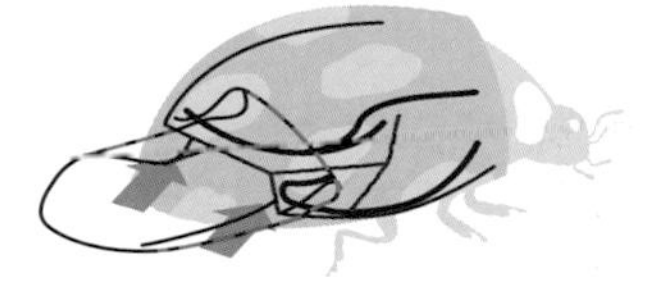

4. As the abdomen moves, the wing folds under the elytron.

5. The wings are now folded into a Z shape and completely under the elytron.

With the resin elytron in place, the team photographed the ladybug's wing retraction again. They also used micro-computed tomography (a micro-CT scan) to make a 3D X-ray image of the folding action. Through these photographs and the X-ray images, they saw the secret to the ladybug's folds—the wing folded across its width and length in mountain and valley folds connected by diamond-shaped crease lines. They also tucked under the elytra in a sort of Z shape. The researchers also discovered how the ladybug uses its body to push its wings into their folded shapes. It pumps its abdomen up and down to move its wings while structures on the underside and edges of its elytra and the top of its abdomen hold the wings in place while they fold. And the researchers found out how the veins help—they bend into a cylindrical shape while the wings fold, acting like coiled springs to hold onto energy. When the elytra uncover the wings again, the veins release their stored energy to pop the ladybug's wings open in a fraction of a second.

Saito thinks the principles behind the ladybug's wing folding can be used in a number of ways to improve technology. Solar arrays and antenna reflectors on satellites might benefit from his research. Even the wings of aircraft that land on carrier ships in the ocean may fold like ladybug wings one day. This means more aircraft could possibly park on the decks of the carriers. But something more ordinary could improve with a springlike action similar to the veins in ladybug wings—umbrellas. Saito believes "beetle wing folding has the potential to change the umbrella design that has been basically unchanged for more than [one thousand] years."

PROTEIN FOLDING

Nature is filled with all kinds of folds, but you don't have to go far to find them. Instead of searching around outside, just look inside yourself. The human body is packed with folds—from our brains to proteins in our cells. As our brains grow, they become wrinkled and folded with grooves of various sizes. These folds seem to have something to do with our intelligence, because not all animals have wrinkly brains. Whales, dolphins, elephants, dogs, and primates have highly folded brains as humans do. Some animals have smaller and smoother brains though, such as mice. Folding helps increase the brain's surface area, which increases the number of neurons. Neurons act as links, where messages from the brain connect to other parts of the brain and the body. Having more links allows the brain to send more messages. Humans' cognitive abilities likely come from our highly folded brains.

Folding is a critical function inside the human body, not only in the brain but also in all of our cells, where tiny proteins perform all kinds of functions. Each protein is made of a string of amino acids. These strings fold up into many different 3D shapes. After they take shape, they begin to function. Some proteins stick to bacteria and

Force Folding

You'd think that dropping heavy books on a paper cone would just destroy it. The force pushes down on the paper, crushing it flat. Yet, take a look at how it crushed, and you'll see it has a folded pattern, one that looks a lot like the spiral on a pine cone. Forces such as gravity and torque create uniform folds too, as Biruta Kresling noticed.

She designed an experiment to show how a natural folding pattern could be made using force. Kresling wrapped thin paper over two cylinders, leaving a gap open between them under the paper. With each hand on a cylinder, she quickly twisted her hands in opposite directions. The paper folded in the gap, making a uniform crease pattern of repeating triangles within quadrilaterals. The pattern was later named the Kresling pattern, but it is also called the triangulated cylinder pattern. Kresling noticed that it looks very similar to something she'd seen in nature: a crease pattern found in the air sac of the hawk moth insect. This pattern has helped engineers design objects that withstand twisting pressure. They incorporate the pattern's creases into their designs of cylinders and tubes.

FORCE FOLDING: DIY

You can replicate Biruta Kresling's experiments with folding using nothing but force. See what patterns are revealed by following these simple instructions:

You'll Need

- protractor
- pencil
- paper
- scissors
- glue
- large, heavy book

Here's How

1. Use the protractor to draw a large circle on the paper. Mark the center of the circle with a pencil.

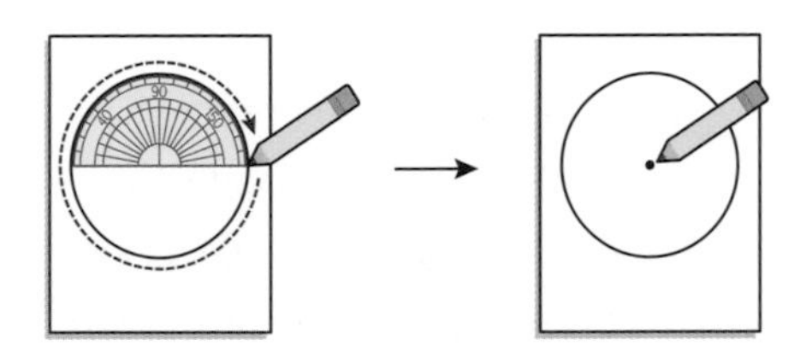

2. Cut out the circle. Cut in from the outer edge to the center to make one cut line.

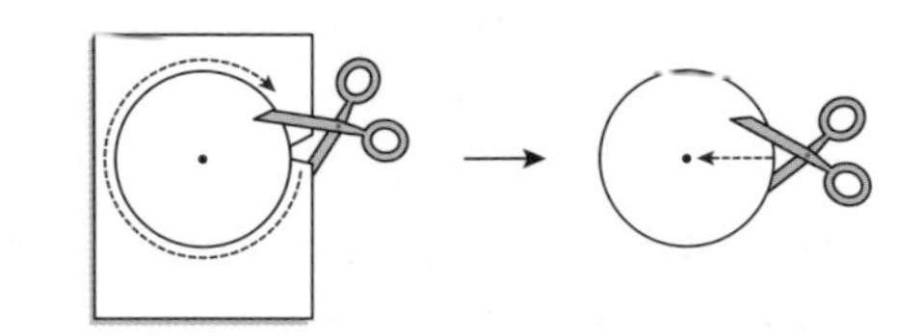

3. Bend the paper at the cut edge to shape the circle into a cone. Then glue the edges in place and let dry.

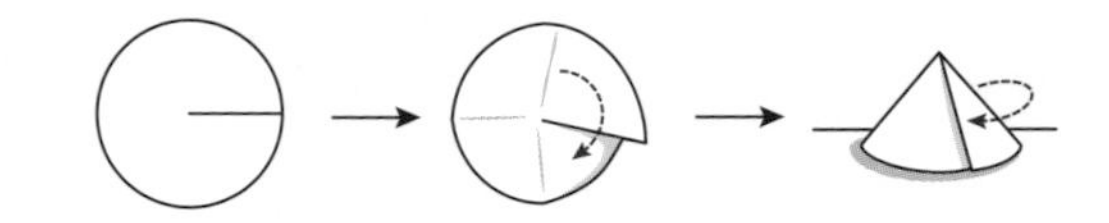

4. Place the cone on a large table, and then drop the book directly over its point.

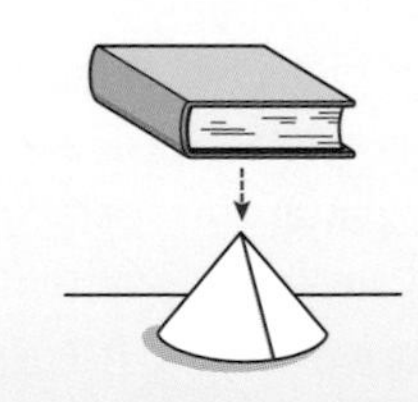

5. Take the cone out, and check out how it looks. You'll see an intricate folded pattern inside the cone. Pull the tip of the cone out to examine the folds more closely. Do they look a bit like the spiral of a pine cone or a seashell?

viruses to protect you from getting sick. Some carry messages with them between cells or to organs to help regulate bodily functions. Others make chemical reactions happen inside cells. And others provide structure to cells or move atoms and molecules from cell to cell in the body. Each protein is made of the same kinds of amino acids arranged in different sequences and folded up in different ways.

Researchers have been trying to create designer proteins that perform specific functions for years, but knowing how they would fold was difficult to predict. In 2016 a paper describing how to create computer programs that can predict how a protein will fold was published by David Baker and Debora Marks. These computational biologists use biological data to create algorithms used in computer programs. Using their algorithms, researchers have designed proteins that could become a universal flu vaccine or that fold into tiny cages that could hold different kinds of medicines or parts of DNA. These protein cages could deliver the medicine or DNA throughout the body to help treat different diseases. This is just the beginning for designer proteins, which could potentially solve many medical problems, and figuring out how they fold is a key to making them a reality.

CHAPTER 3
THE LANGUAGE OF FOLDING:
Origami Math

There's visual beauty in a folded origami art piece—it elegantly models a piece of nature, a creature, or a beautiful geometric design. There's also an elegance and beauty in origami that we can't immediately understand with our eyes: the mathematics behind the folds. Folding engineers like Robert Lang recognize the importance of this mathematical language. Origami's "patterns, relationships, wherever they are found in the natural world, in the technological world . . . can be described, and, very often, mathematics is the language that describes them both concisely and precisely," he says. This language of mathematics connects the art form to other fields—technology, engineering, architecture, furniture and clothing design, and more—that also use mathematics.

One branch of math that origami is obviously connected to is geometry: the shapes, angles, and vertices you can see in the crease patterns of an unfolded piece. But what's less obvious is that origami is also filled with almost every other kind of mathematics. According to Western New England University professor and origami math researcher Thomas Hull, "There is also combinatorics, which is a branch of math that deals with counting things . . . [and] other branches of mathematics that have applications in origami include algebra, trigonometry, calculus, differential geometry, and topology. Even complex numbers are useful for studying origami!" Origami is a great example of how many branches of math can intersect and overlap.

FINDING ORIGAMI'S MATH

Few people seriously studied origami's mathematical properties until the 1980s. Before then a research paper or book here and there illuminated some of the mathematical properties of folding, but not much came of them, and they never connected to bigger ideas about folding and origami. According to Hull, people first started studying the geometry of paper folding in the nineteenth century. German educator Friedrich Froebel was one of the first of those scholars.

Nature's Math

As a language that describes patterns, math is found in art, science, technology . . . and also nature. Just look around you, and you'll see patterns everywhere: the number of petals on a flower, the seeds inside an apple, even a spiraling nautilus seashell or a galaxy in space that gets bigger and bigger at the same ratio.

Even inside a beehive, bees are unknowingly making math. Their honeycomb is all about geometry: each cell has the same hexagonal shape. And each side of each hexagon is exactly the same length. A honeycomb also has something in common with some origami patterns: it is a naturally occurring tessellation that provides a strong structure while minimizing the amount of materials needed to build it.

Another natural pattern is the Fibonacci sequence, which was originally described in India in 600 CE. In 1202 Italian mathematician Leonardo of Pisa told the Western world about the sequence in his book *Liber abaci*. The sequence is a series of numbers in which each number is the sum of the previous two numbers. It goes like this: 1, 1, 2, 3, 5, 8, 13, 21, 34, 55, and so on.

What's incredible is that these numbers often appear in nature. For instance, if you count the petals on a variety of flowers, you'll find different Fibonacci numbers: an iris has three petals, a wild rose has five, a black-eyed Susan has twenty-one, and a Michaelmas daisy has fifty-five or eighty-nine. Count the seed spirals on a sunflower's head, and you'll see 21, 34, 55, 89, or 144 clockwise spirals paired with 34, 55, 89, 144, or 233 counterclockwise spirals, respectively—all Fibonacci numbers. Keep looking and you'll see more and more examples of Fibonacci numbers in nature: the branches that split off a tree trunk and the spirals on a pineapple or a pine cone.

His innovative ideas changed education and introduced kindergarten to schools in the 1830s. Froebel believed young children should begin to learn through structured play, and so he designed a series of play objects he called "gifts" to give children. One of these gifts was a package of squares of colored paper and diagrams and instructions for folding them, meant to help children learn about shapes, symmetry, and geometry. "Froebel's influence caused math teachers around the world to start thinking about origami and geometry—that is, thinking

The Fibonacci sequence is found in interesting and beautiful patterns of flora and fauna, such as this sunflower.

It's almost eerie how often these numbers pop up in the natural world. Some scientists believe the spirals and spacing are a by-product of the way plants have evolved to maximize stem space, but no one knows for certain why the sequence appears so frequently in nature.

about how you can use origami to construct geometric objects," says Hull, "in the same way that the classic tools of straightedge and compass are used to construct geometric things."

Froebel's influence reached India, where mathematician Tandalam Sundara Row built upon Froebel's ideas. In 1893 Row wrote the book *Geometric Exercises in Paper Folding.* This book was later published by a British publishing company and then reprinted in different parts of the world, including the United States. It described paper-folding exercises that could be used to teach geometry, and the book influenced more people to begin studying these ideas.

In the 1930s, Italian mathematician Margherita Beloch found that origami could even solve seemingly impossible ancient math problems. The one she worked on was the Delian problem, an ancient Greek question that asks, How do you double the volume of a cube? The answer would take the form of a mathematical equation so that no matter the original size of the cube, you could always use the equation to double its volume. One restriction given by ancient Greek philosopher Plato was that the answer had to be found using a straightedge and a compass, his preferred tools for geometry. No Greek could find the answer with this restriction. Ancient Egyptians also tried, but did not succeed. The question remained unsolvable with the original restrictions until Beloch tried a different approach: folding a square piece of paper. Using her folding technique, she showed how origami could be a more powerful geometric tool than a straightedge and compass. Peter Messer later found a different paper-folding method that also answered this ancient question. Although Beloch had found the geometric answer, it went mostly unnoticed.

More than forty years later, David Huffman, a mathematician, computer science pioneer, and UC–Santa Cruz professor, published a paper on the geometry of curves and paper folding. Known mostly for developing Huffman coding (an algorithm that uses 1s and 0s to best represent numbers, letters, and symbols according to their frequency of use, a process which compresses data so that it is easier to store and transmit, such as ZIP and GIF files), Huffman was also an avid origamist and a pioneer in curved-crease folding. His 1976 paper, titled *Curvature and Creases: A Primer on Paper*, described the fundamentals of both curved and straight creases used in paper folding as well as how they interact with each other. In 1977 Scottish mathematician Stewart Robertson published his study of the geometry of paper folding titled *Isometric Folding of Riemannian Manifolds*. In it he describes some mathematical properties of origami after studying the seemingly random creases made by crumpling a piece of paper. He found that the creases were not random and that they followed certain mathematical rules. While both mathematicians made important observations about paper folding, their papers remained fairly obscure until the 1980s and 1990s, when the idea of origami mathematics was born at the first OSME conference in 1989.

ORIGAMI THEOREMS AND AXIOMS

In the 1980s, several mathematicians developed theorems and axioms for how paper can be folded, which became the mathematical laws of flat origami (origami that can be flattened without adding any additional crease lines). Mathematician and origami artist Humiaki Huzita presented a set of six axioms (proven mathematical statements) at the First International Meeting of Origami Science and Technology. The axioms describe six ways to create a crease using existing points and lines on a piece of paper. Mathematicians Koshiro Hatori and Jacques Justin then discovered a seventh axiom. These seven axioms were later called the Huzita-Justin or Huzita-Hatori axioms. They showed there were many geometric possibilities within paper folding.

In addition to these axioms, there are four fundamental laws that origami must follow. One of these laws is called the Two-Colorability Law (figure 1). The law states that if you color an origami crease

Figure 1

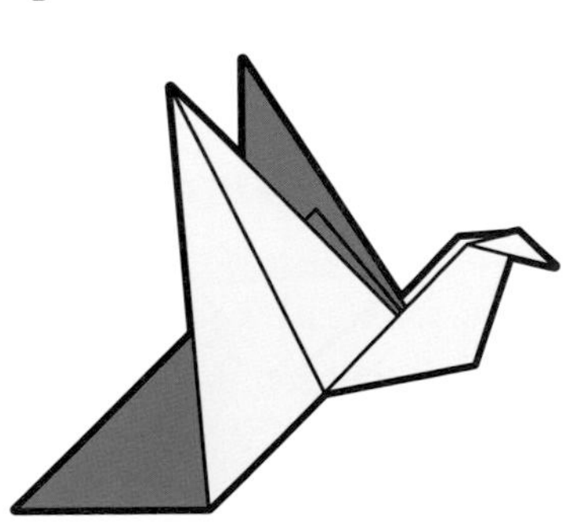

pattern with two colors, the same color won't ever touch itself when folded at the crease—it will always touch the other color. The crease pattern will always have alternating colors between the creases, sort of like a checkerboard.

The Two-Colorability Law relates to a second law called Maekawa's Theorem (figure 2). This law was named after origami artist and mathematician Jun Maekawa, who first described this property of origami. It explains that the number of mountain and valley folds that meet at any vertex (angular point) in an origami piece will always differ by a quanitity of two. Imagine you have a circle of paper and make some folds around a vertex at its center. Both mountain and valley folds meet at the vertex. Fold it as many times as you like, and then unfold it. Count the number of mountain folds and then the number of valley folds. Their total number may vary, but their proportion always stays the same—they always differ by two.

Japanese mathematician and origamist Toshikazu Kawasaki is well known for one of his most famous origami designs: the Kawasaki Rose. It uses a curling technique that makes the paper look like overlapping rose petals on a bud. Kawasaki is also known for defining another origami law, called Kawasaki's Theorem (figure 3). It describes the angles that meet at a vertex. Creases create angular sections within

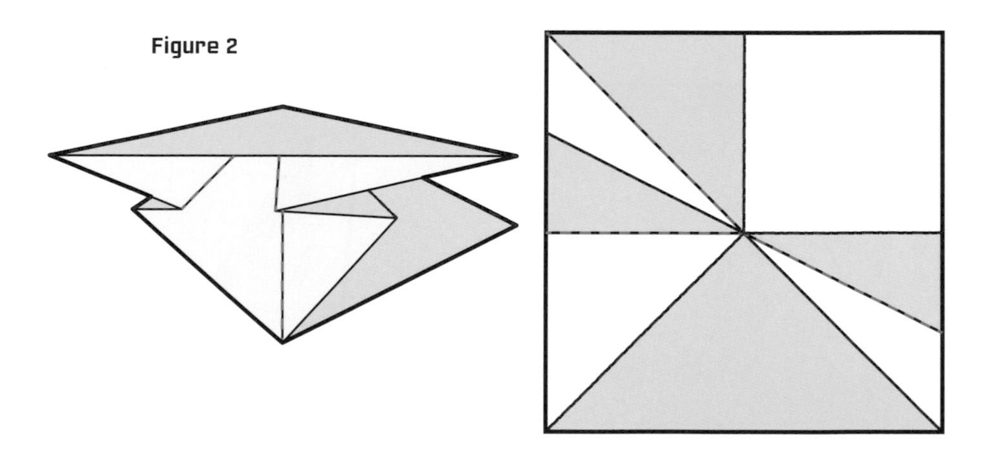
Figure 2

the circle: from one crease to the next is an angle. If you add all the angles up around a vertex, they will equal 360 degrees: the angle of a full circle. Each section has an angle that is less than 360 degrees. Kawasaki's Theorem states that if you add up the opposite angles around that vertex, they will equal 180 degrees: the angle of a straight line. For example, if a folded piece of paper had six sections around a vertex, you could number them going clockwise around the vertex (1, 2, 3, 4, 5, 6). Then if you measured the angles of each, you'd see that angles 1, 3, and 5 added together to 180 degrees. Angles 2, 4, and 6 added together would also equal 180 degrees. Add them all together, and you'd have 360 degrees.

Jacques Justin worked out the final major origami theorem, called Justin's Non-crossing Conditions. It looks at what a flat folded origami piece might look like if you cut through it, creating a cross section. Looking at the layers, you'd see creases and flat sections. The theorem states what you won't find—a flat section that goes through a crease, no matter how many creases or flat sections there are. The creases can overlap each other and the sections can stack, but the two cannot intersect.

Figure 3

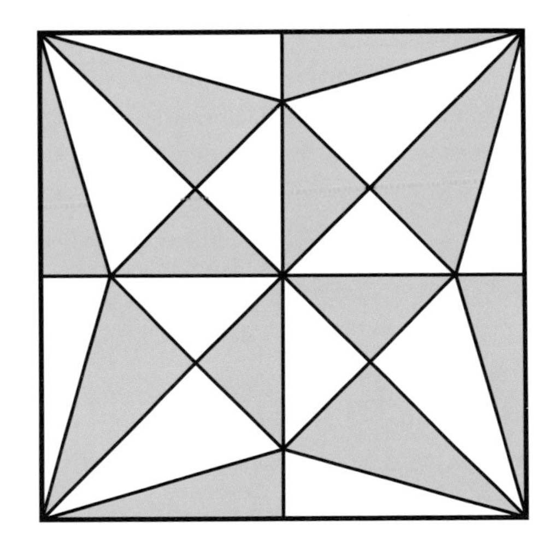

Thomas Hull: Creases, PHiZZ, and Origami Fun

Thomas Hull's love for origami and math started when he was just eight years old. "There was something about following the origami instructions to end up with a cool object that appealed to me," Hull says. One of his early memories with origami happened when he was around ten years old. After folding a crane or some similar piece, he didn't keep it to admire—he unfolded it. Hull wanted to see the creases the folds made. "Looking at those creases, I thought, 'There is definitely some math or geometry happening here.' That is, it was clear to me that the creases had to follow some rules in order to fold up into the shape I had made. I didn't know what those rules were, but certainly there was something going on there."

Continuing his origami hobby, Hull eventually attended college where he studied mathematics. While in college, he discovered some advanced origami books that mentioned different origami theorems found by Japanese origamists, yet the books didn't describe them in enough detail. This sparked his curiosity, so Hull hunted down all the papers he could find on these theorems. But there were only a few, and Hull "was left to try to discover the proofs of these origami theorems on [his] own." In doing this, he found that the origami theorems "were really elegant and beautiful!" he says.

Hull went on to become an associate professor of mathematics at Western New England University, where he teaches college-level mathematics and also does origami math research. For his research, Hull collaborates with other mathematicians, engineers, and physicists to understand how paper folding works. He's an accomplished author who's written papers and books on origami math. Hull is also famous for his modular origami creations. Modular origami uses multiple pieces of paper to make geometric objects that Hull says look "really pretty." Two especially famous designs are Hull's Five Intersecting Tetrahedra model and his Pentagon-Hexagon Zig-Zag (PHiZZ) unit. There are tons of videos and instructions online for how to make Hull's designs. He even won an award from the British Origami Society for his Five Intersecting Tetrahedra model—in 2000 the society honored Hull's work as being one of the "top 10 origami models of all time."

ORIGAMI GETS DIGITAL

The theorems and axioms described in the 1980s and 1990s are some of the mathematical basics of folding origami. In the late 1990s, some origamists turned to computers to research what else origami could do.

Thomas Hull shows off some of his origami creations.

With Tomohiro Tachi, Hull is researching self-folding origami. This kind of origami utilizes different mechanisms, from motors to chemical reactions within materials, to induce self-folding. He's also writing a book on origami mathematics as an entire field. As a professor, Hull tries to take the fear out of math and reveal its beauty. As a researcher, he finds that "exploring mathematical questions that no one knows the answer to, or questions that no one has ever thought to ask before, is a thrill and a joy." Sharing his love for mathematics and origami has been an extremely rewarding career, and from early on he decided to "make it my mission to share the math of origami with the rest of the world, since it seemed that very few people know about it. I've been working on that mission ever since!"

Thomas Hull recounts that theoretical computer scientists began asking questions such as, "Given a set of crease lines, how easy is it to tell if they can be folded flat?" or "If I want to fold a piece of paper to make it look like a certain insect, can I devise an algorithm that tells me how to do that?" By using computer programs, these scientists could begin to answer their questions. Programs could create complex origami designs that result in folded pieces unlike anything seen before.

Robert J. Lang began working on his computer program, called TreeMaker, in the early 1990s. After Lang developed the first version of TreeMaker, his origami skills improved. He added new algorithms to the program and released updated versions of the software. By 1998 TreeMaker 4.0 was up and running and was now a powerful origami creation tool. Lang was able to create patterns on it that he could never design by hand. He used it to help design several complicated pieces, including a scorpion with eight legs and a raised tail called *Scorpion Varileg, Opus 379*, and a lobster with a segmented tail and raised antennae called *Maine Lobster, Opus 447*. The most recent software version came out in 2005, and anyone can find it on Lang's website for free. To start, users draw a stick figure on-screen that looks like a horse, a cat, or whatever they'd like to create. The program then computes a crease pattern, which users can print out and then fold.

While working on TreeMaker 5.0, Lang consulted with Erik Demaine and Erik's fellow mathematician and father, Martin Demaine. Erik Demaine had been working on his own origami algorithms since he was an eighteen-year-old PhD student at the University of Waterloo in Canada. He was researching whether it was possible to make any imaginable 3D shape with origami. In 1999 he developed an algorithm that could explore this question, but it wasn't perfect. You could make any shape, but you had to use one long, thin, continuous piece of paper. And the finished folded pieces were not very sturdy. Demaine continued working on his algorithm with Tomohiro Tachi, a University of Tokyo associate professor in graphic and computer sciences. By 2017 the team had worked out the kinks and developed a new and much more efficient algorithm. The algorithm designs origami pieces as polyhedrons, with many flat facets covering the surface of the shape. Demaine and Tachi added the algorithm to Tachi's software, called Origamizer. Users input

Studying Mathematics: Hull's Advice

When asked if he had any advice or thoughts about being an innovative mathematician, here's what Hull had to say:

> No, actually. Most mathematicians, myself included, suffer from big cases of imposter syndrome, probably because as you train to become a mathematician, you get used to being wrong all the time. There's nothing like math to put your ego in check—math will continuously show you how your ideas don't work and challenge [you] to try and try again until you finally figure out what's going on.
>
> I never think of myself as an innovative mathematician! But I *love, love, love* math. I also *love, love, love* origami. And I feel extremely lucky that I get to do math and origami as part of my career as a professor. But math is brutal. It really helps to be passionate about math in order to put up with how hard it is. Doing math requires persistence and hard work. Most mathematicians are not natural geniuses for whom it all comes easily. No, we just work really hard and never give up. But for me, I'm working on things I love, and it's really fun! So I've learned to live with the fact that I often feel like I don't understand anything.
>
> The only advice I can give is to be brave [and] not give up! So much of learning math is psychological. If you convince yourself that there's no way that you can solve a certain problem, then you definitely won't solve it because you're giving up before you even try. It takes courage to make yourself not just turn away from a hard problem, but to instead think to yourself, 'Well, what can I do? Can I try an easier case? Or can I try playing with examples to see how the problem works?' Making yourself persist and think of strategies you can take is mental training, not math training, but it's equally (if not more) important as simply learning math.

the finished shape they would like to fold (such as a bunny) and the program creates a crease pattern for them to fold into that shape.

Computational origami is a powerful tool. Originally made to create origami designs, the software is packed with potential for materials other than paper. But folding with thicker materials is tricky, so engineers have to figure out how to translate the folding patterns made for paper to those for much thicker metal and other materials.

CHAPTER 4

FOLDING THICK:

Engineering Origami

How do you go from folded paper to folded solar panels? It's not as easy as just taking a crease pattern and printing it onto metal. Paper is so thin that it's described as having zero thickness, and that's the material that most origami designs are created for. You need a certain kind of origami pattern to fold thicker materials—patterns that can make rigid origami. "Rigid origami is when you fold a piece of paper trying to keep all of the parts of the paper rigidly flat as you fold, so that the paper only bends at the creases," says Hull. It keeps sections flat and can easily fold up into its finished form and then unfold so that it's flat again, all without distorting the pattern.

This is the kind of origami that engineers love, because rigid origami crease patterns work well with sheet metal, hard plastic, or other stiff materials. Instead of creases, engineers use hinges and other methods to make the folds. Rigid origami has many engineering advantages. In most manufacturing, workers make a mold and then pour liquified materials into the mold. The materials harden to the shape needed. To change the finished product, you need to make a new mold, which can be costly and time-consuming, as well as limiting: each mold makes one shape. But a folding pattern can be used on flat materials and to change the final product, you just need to change the pattern. No molds are needed, and one-off designs can be made cheaply and quickly.

Rigid origami is also interesting to architects. They could use it to make walls, ceilings, and facades that move to transform a space—for instance, the Al Bahr Towers in Abu Dhabi, United Arab Emirates, have a folding facade that changes shape in response to the sun, shading the building from intense sunlight when the facade is unfolded. Rigid origami can make buildings easier to construct and make lightweight materials—which are easier to build with, cheaper to buy, and make more efficient use of space—achieve a sturdiness not otherwise possible.

To turn a rigid origami pattern meant for paper into a pattern that works for thick materials, you have to rethink the design

An Origami Chapel

When the nuns of St. Loup, a religious community in Switzerland, needed a new residence in 2007, they had to find a temporary place to worship during its construction. The architects estimated the new residence could take eighteen months or more to complete, and there weren't a lot of funds for a temporary chapel. The nuns considered several options, including using a tentlike structure or renting space in another building. Instead, the architects proposed designing and building a temporary chapel. It could be made cheaply with preassembled panels and then disassembled and reused somewhere else when the nuns no longer needed it. The nuns agreed, and the architecture firm LOCALARCHITECTURE designed it. The architects teamed up with a Swiss research institute and university with a program that specializes in timber-frame construction and that had been experimenting with building designs inspired by origami.

They modeled the structure using folded paper. It had a corrugated shape, with walls and a roof that zigzagged in and out. The shape made for excellent acoustics inside the building—sound bounced off the angled walls. The angled walls also helped diffuse light within the chapel. The final structure was made from prefabricated timber panels with folded steel plates screwed in where the panels met. From the entrance, the chapel roof rose up toward the opposite end, where clear plastic panels looked a lot like stained glass. The team was able to create the design and build the beautiful and reusable chapel in a quick three months.

without changing its folding properties. Mathematics and origami software provide the keys to unlocking origami and making it work for thick materials.

CREATING HANAFLEX

After receiving one of the National Science Foundation's ODISSEI grants in 2012, a team of researchers at Brigham Young University (BYU) led by Professor Larry L. Howell joined up with NASA JPL engineer Brian Trease and Robert J. Lang to focus on designing folding solar panels based on origami. They decided to use an origami design called the

Architects designed the temporary chapel using a computer program and then sent that information to machines that cut the required shapes out of timber. The temporary chapel remains standing as of February 2020.

flasher as their basis for the technological design. Although many people independently discovered and analyzed the concept of flashers, several flasher designs well known in the origami community were created by professional origamists Jeremy Shafer and Chris Palmer. This design coils around a cylindrical core in a helix and then, when someone pulls on two opposing corners, spreads out into a large flat square.

To go from the flasher design to a design that accommodated thickness, the team needed to modify it with math. Lang and the team wrote algorithms to change the flasher design with a computer program. Using their computer model, the team developed a solar

Shannon Zirbel, a PhD student in mechanical engineering at Brigham Young University, Provo, Utah, unfolds a solar panel array that was designed using the principles of origami. She worked on this project with Brian Trease at NASA's Jet Propulsion Laboratory, Pasadena, California.

array made of thick panels that fold at hinges along its "crease" lines. The team then created physical models based on the design. The result was a scaled prototype of a solar array that could fold down to 8.9 feet (2.7 m) in diameter and unfold to become 82 feet (25 m) across. This kind of array could fit around a spacecraft inside a rocket. Once the spacecraft is deployed from the rocket in space, the array can easily unfold around it.

The team published their findings in 2013 in the *Journal of Mechanical Design*. They called the solar array HanaFlex (*hana* is Japanese for "flower") because it looks like a flower opening up when it is deployed. Trease said this work will help NASA develop solar-powered thrusters that spacecraft can use to move or change direction. And having solar panels that encircle a spacecraft, rather than stick out at its sides like arms (as they do on some spacecraft), may help with its stability as it floats through space.

RIGID DESIGNS

Most origami patterns aren't right for rigid origami. Folders need to twist, bend, or curve the paper before it reaches its finished state. The challenge is finding an origami pattern that can work with materials that do not deform as they fold. The Miura-ori is one of the most standard kinds of rigid origami used in structures and structural design, which can be altered to make different shapes and curves. Other tessellations also translate well into structural design.

To see if an origami pattern can become a rigid origami design, researchers need to test it mathematically. They often do this by creating a model. One model they might use is the matrix model. This model uses a single, fixed vertex with folds emanating from the vertex. One condition for the model to work as rigid origami takes some imagination: picture yourself walking along the folds around a vertex, making a complete circle around that point. If you returned to the same spot where you started, the design would work as rigid origami. Another model called the Gaussian curvature model maps the curves on a surface. This model can tell researchers if the surfaces remain rigid while the crease areas move.

Researchers also have to think about how the folds will work in rigid origami. Engineers have developed several different methods to fold thick materials along crease lines, and each has some benefits and issues.

- The **hinge shift** method adjusts where the hinges are placed at the folds between panels. They are put at either the top or bottom of the panel's edges, on the valley edges of the fold, rather than at the centers of the edges. This allows the surfaces of the panels to flatten against one another, but a drawback is that the folding motion is limited.
- The **volume trimming** method thins the panels at their edges. This allows the hinges to have more motion than the hinge shift method, but the panels need to have a slanted shape. This shape can be difficult to make on a large scale.

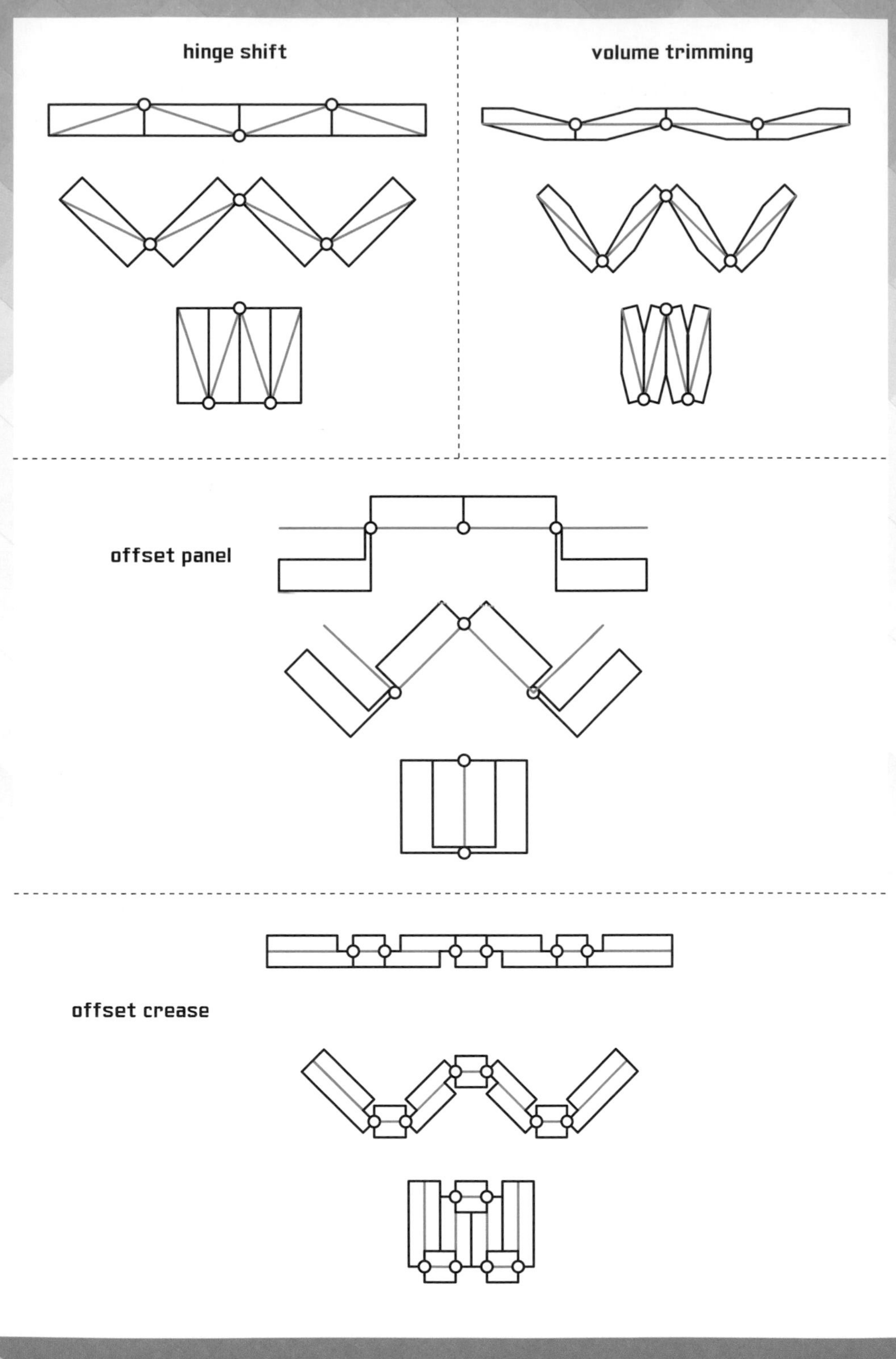
hinge shift
volume trimming
offset panel
offset crease

- The **offset panel** method allows for the best range of motion. At each fold, a hinge sits at the edge of one panel. The other panel leaves the folding plane open, and the thick material sits to the side. This allows it to fold around the panel next to it, but it can also be difficult to manufacture.
- The **offset crease** method uses a small portion of the thick material with hinges at each side. The hinges connect to the larger panels, which also have cutout areas to allow for the thick material used at the crease. Other methods allow panels to slide along the crease lines.

Researchers continue to experiment with crease methods for rigid origami that allow for the best movement and are easy to manufacture.

SIMULATIONS, TUBES, AND SELF-FOLDING

Tomohiro Tachi is at the forefront of developments in rigid origami. He has been exploring ways that rigid origami can be used in architecture and engineering. One of the tools he developed to explore the properties of rigid origami is software called the Rigid Origami Simulator. This software follows the matrix model to test origami designs. It allows users to experiment with the geometries of a design and see how it might fold and unfold. One rigid origami structure that Tachi has helped design is based on the Miura-ori. It is a tube made from two interlocking zigzag-shaped tubes. Each zigzag tube is flexible on its own, but when zippered together they become very strong and stiff. The zippered tube can extend and fold flat and could be made with sheet metal or thin plastic. Working with University of Illinois at Urbana-Champaign then graduate student Evgueni Filipov and Georgia Tech professor Glaucio Paulino, Tachi and his team published their findings in 2016. They imagine this kind of tube could be used on a robotic arm, to build an emergency shelter, or even become pop-up furniture. This is just one of many rigid origami research projects Tachi is involved with.

Ron Resch: Tessellation Visionary

In the early 1960s, Ron Resch was among the few people who explored the connection between folding and architecture. A visionary artist and computer scientist, he began his research by studying crumpled paper for his University of Iowa master of fine arts thesis—a film titled *Paper and Stick Film*. He noticed the geometric shapes that the random crumples formed and mapped them out using a pen. Using the shapes he found (which he called modules), he created tessellations of repeating modules. Before computers had such capabilities, Resch designed, hand-built, and tested tessellation models from paper to see how they could move and what kinds of forms they could take. Then, in the early days of the computer, he invented the code for programs that could visualize 3D objects on screens. He predicted that computers could one day be used to model, test, and modify origami designs, speeding up the creative process. This prediction came true with Origamizer, TreeMaker, and other design programs.

Resch also experimented with tessellation patterns that could be used in architecture. One of his designs in the late 1960s was for a self-supporting dome made from a tessellated pattern. Resch also created a tessellation pattern for a tube. He made large, room-size domes folded from single sheets of paper. His triangle fold pattern has been the basis for different adaptive and flexible surfaces, from ceiling acoustic panels that can be adjusted to perfect sound resonance in a room to the adjustable building facade on the Al Bahr Towers in Abu Dhabi. Resch's unusual and visionary patterns continue to inspire origami artists, architects, and engineers, and his thesis film is an essential part of any serious origami engineer's education.

A tessellation is a repeating pattern of interlocking shapes.

Tachi has also been working with Hull on self-folding rigid origami. "Whenever an engineer designs an origami mechanism that is supposed to fold on its own, without the aid of human hands, we can describe it as 'self-folding,'" explains Hull. "That is, the material has to have some way of making the creases fold." Motors or springs might help the structure fold, or maybe the material tightens or swells at the hinges to fold. Regardless of how a structure self-folds, the researchers want to control which way it folds. That's the big challenge Tachi and Hull are facing. Their work focuses on "ways to program the crease activation methods to ensure that the whole pattern will fold like we want it to," says Hull. "What I hope to do is work with some materials physicists . . . to take the mathematical models of self-folding that Tachi and I are developing and see if they can work in real-life materials."

HEART STENTS AND PAPER BAGS

Professor and researcher Zhong You is also at the cutting edge of rigid-folding technology. He's been experimenting with rigid origami at the Department of Engineering Science at Oxford University in England since the 1990s. Yet unlike other origami engineers, You didn't like origami as a child. Growing up in China, he learned how to fold some simple origami designs. "It was all about how to fold a frog or something else that was pretty but had no use," You told *Science Magazine*. "Also, I was no good at it!" But as a civil engineer years later, You changed his mind about origami when he realized its engineering potential. Some of his engineering inspiration comes from everyday folded packaging—a crushable beverage can from Tokyo with a diamond-shaped folding pattern and a paper bag he picked up in Boston. These objects have given him ideas for rocket and silo structures and medical and packaging applications.

As a team, You and his student Kaori Kuribayashi-Shigetomi are using origami to help save lives. They developed a medical device that can help prevent heart attacks—a deployable heart stent.

In-Depth Tech: Robotic Grabber for Deep-Sea Creatures

Folding technology is helping humans explore space. It's also helping humans explore one of the least-known places on our planet—the deep sea. Down at the bottom of the ocean are bizarre, delicate organisms, such as a spaghettilike animal related to jellyfish and glowing bioluminescent octopuses, which look nothing like the creatures we know. They exist in harsh environments that lack sunlight and oxygen and where there aren't many plants. Scientists estimate that there are more than one million undiscovered creatures at the deepest parts of the ocean. People need to travel in high-tech submarines or operate remote-controlled ones equipped with robotic arms that can withstand the deep sea's high pressures to see and study these creatures of the deep.

And even for use in the deep sea, origami is inspiring the technology scientists use to study the strange creatures they find, many of which have soft, jellylike bodies. They require delicate handling, so that's what makes the rotary-actuated dodecahedron (RAD) sampler ideal for these sample-collecting deep-sea missions. Previous grabbing technology was made for mining purposes, such as sucking up silt or picking up rocks, and it harms and kills soft-bodied creatures. The RAD does not. It can safely enclose an animal while scientists photograph and study it, and then release it back into the ocean unharmed. RAD uses a self-folding polyhedra design initiated by one small motor.

The side panels of the RAD sampler are mostly made of pentagon-shaped, 3D-printed plastic components. The final closing piece is made of smaller triangular sections. The side panels are separated into five arms that connect at a central axis, which is also connected to the motor. When the motor initiates a twisting action, the panels fold together. They make a twelve-sided 3D container that can trap creatures, along with seawater, safely inside. Each panel is edged with a soft silicone to help seal the container better, make it last longer, and minimize any damage to soft-bodied creatures. Scientists have tested the RAD sampler in the ocean to capture soft-bodied creatures and envision it being used in other ways too—for deployable habitats such as pop-up, self-folding living spaces for astronauts living on colonies on other planets; space solar arrays; and even tiny electronic and mechanical systems.

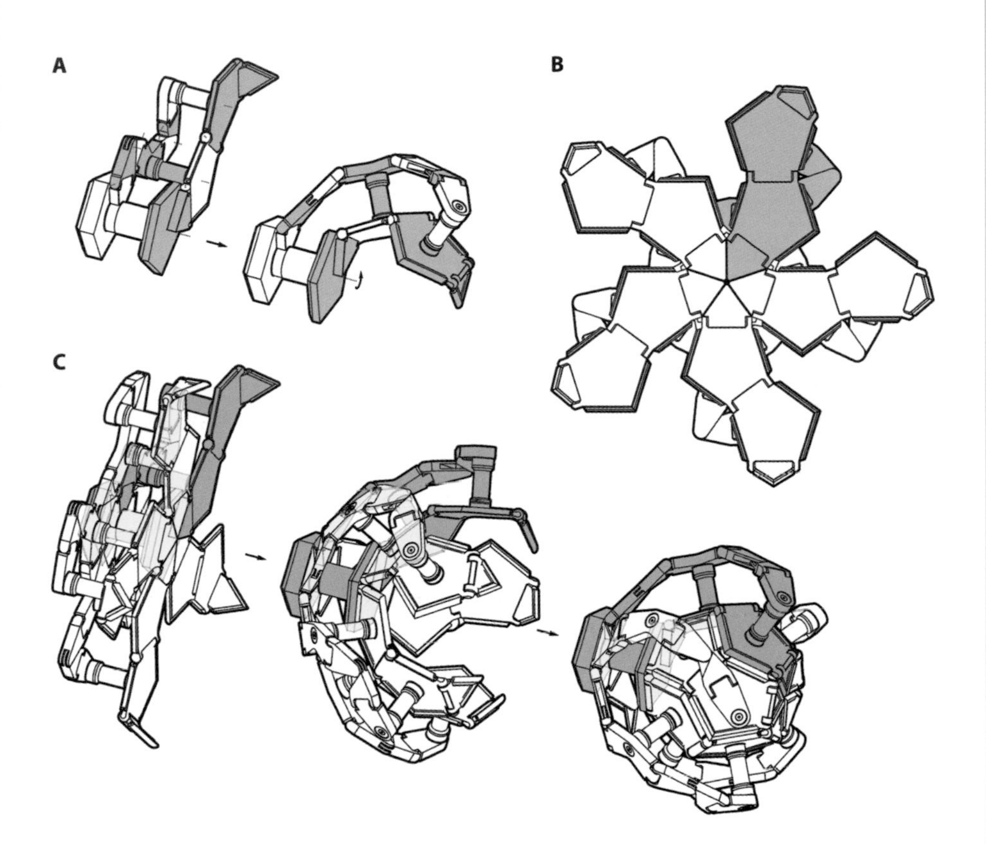

This diagram illustrates how the RAD folds shut. In part A, a single arm folds shut. Part B shows how this arm fits into an arrangement with the other four. Part C shows how all the arms fold together to create an enclosed space.

Heart stents have been in use since the mid-1980s. They are devices inserted into an artery, a blood vessel that carries blood filled with oxygen from the heart to the rest of the body. Arteries can become clogged with fat, calcium, or other substances found in blood in certain areas over time that slow blood flow. Clogged arteries can eventually lead to heart attacks or strokes. To prevent that from happening, doctors insert a heart stent into clogged arteries. The stent props open clogged arteries, increasing the blood flow. Typical heart stents are tubes made from wire mesh and are inserted in a collapsed form into the artery. Then a balloon inflates to expand the stent and lock it in place. It works, but there are a few problems with the design: tissue can grow in through the mesh holes, and the stents can slip out of place. With a fabric covering over the mesh, tissue cannot grow through, but the covering reduces friction, meaning the stents can slip out of place. The fabric can also detach. You and Kuribayashi-Shigetomi designed a stent that has a solid surface and no covering. It enters the artery in a folded state and, when unfolded, the stent snaps into place. The team based their design on

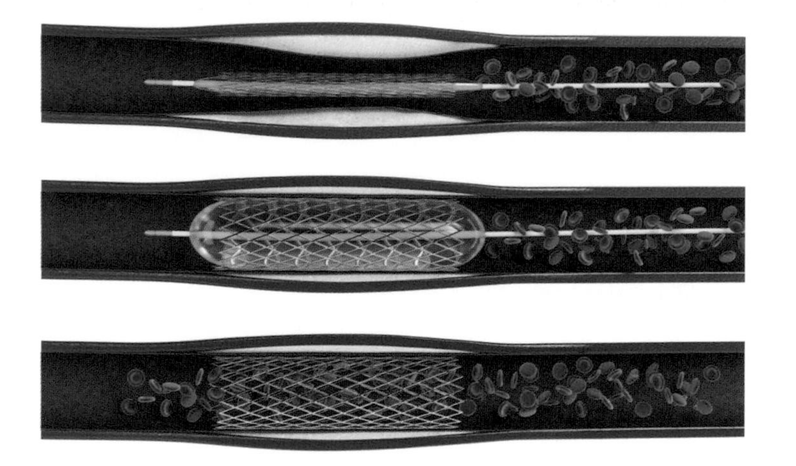

This diagram illustrates how a foldable heart stent might be inserted into a blood vessel, unfold, and allow blood cells to flow through a previously clogged region.

patterns used to make cucumber and pineapple origami and created prototypes out of stainless steel and then self-folding materials. The self-folding material activates with heat inside the body and grows to its full diameter as it unfolds inside the artery. The researchers are still testing and developing this new kind of origami stent.

You is also interested in how origami can optimize packaging design. He and research student Weina Wu created a grocery bag made from steel that can fold completely flat. Currently, manufacturers use paper bags folded in this way (which are not very strong) and cardboard boxes (which fold flat but need to be sealed with tape or staples to hold their unfolded shape). His prototype shows that a rigid material could be used to make a box that is sealed on one end. "The packaging industry is the one place people have traditionally thought deeply about paper-folding techniques, and this could really speed up factory assembly lines," You says.

You and Tachi are origami engineers experimenting with the ways rigid origami can help solve engineering problems. Their research and prototypes are inspiring countless others interested in the field. What will their new ideas lead to? A future filled with folds.

CHAPTER 5
OUR FOLDABLE FUTURE:
What's Next in Origami Technology

The seemingly simple art form of origami is influencing the future of technology in important ways and has become deeply immersed in mainstream culture around the world. In 2012 the Japanese American National Museum in Los Angeles, California, was the first museum to show a traveling exhibition highlighting the connections between origami, math, science, and design. It was called *Folding Paper: The Infinite Possibilities of Origami*, with Robert J. Lang as a contributing artist and one of its main advisers. The museum's exhibition brought together forty-five different artists, scientists, and mathematicians from sixteen countries, including Japan, the United States, Uruguay, and Russia. It included more than 150 works that involved folding, which were on display from March 10 through August 26, 2012. The works showed the immense diversity of folded objects as well as the folders that made them. The exhibit also covered the history of origami, origami made to look like real and imagined objects, modular origami showing geometric designs, and origami's impact on science, industry, fashion, and more.

The exhibit included well-known masters of the art, such as Akira Yoshizawa, whose pieces were part of the history of origami, as well as a tiny crane folded from a candy wrapper by Sadako Sasaki, the girl whose story started the Peace Crane Project around the world. Realistic pieces included delicately gilled mushrooms folded by Vincent Floderer; a lifelike pangolin (an armadillo-like animal, covered in curved scales) and a mask of a man with wildly curly hair folded by Eric Joisel; and an emperor scorpion by Lang. Geometric pieces included intricate interlocking shapes folded by Tom Hull, Miyuki Kawamura, and Daniel Kwan. The impact of origami on science, technology, and design included prototypes and videos of futuristic origami applications. You and Kuribayashi-Shigetomi's heart stent, a collapsible dome tent, and a display on Miura's solar array, along with videos about Lang's folded car airbag and telescope lens, showed some of origami's current and potential technological and practical uses. The exhibition even included origami-inspired fashion—a red evening gown made by Los Angeles-based designer Monica Leigh Rodriguez that was inspired by an origami box crane and an off-the-shoulder dress with matching shoes made by Linda Tomoko Mihara, each made from one sheet of folded white parchment paper.

DESIGNS OF THE FUTURE

After its debut at the Japanese American National Museum, the exhibition traveled to museums around the United States until 2016. One of its stops was at the BYU Museum of Art in Provo, Utah. The university was one of the recipients of the National Science Foundation's ODISSEI $2 million grants. Through this grant, Professor Larry L. Howell and graduate students have done innovative work showing how origami and technology intersect. This work, along with the *Folding Paper* exhibit, inspired the school to publish the 2017 book *Y Origami? Explorations in Folding.*

In the book are some of the latest prototypes in the still-emerging field of origami engineering and design. The designs range from space structures to police barricades and foldable furniture, showing how folding can improve both function and the aesthetics. The police barricade is based on a geometric design created by David Huffman. Made of Kevlar (a strong synthetic fabric that's used in bulletproof vests), aluminum, and nylon, the barricade easily unfolds from a flat U shape into a tall barrier that police can crouch behind to shield themselves from bullets. Somewhat similar to the police barrier is a folding temporary shelter large enough for a person to sleep inside, called the Oruga shelter. Other designs include folding felt stools inspired by folding solar panel arrays and a table that has legs that unfold to lie as a flat circle.

TINY ROBOTS, DRUG DELIVERY, AND MICROTOOLS

BYU's book highlights some of the latest designs in origami engineering. Some are still in the prototype stage, and some are

DIY Origami: Learning the Basics

Want to try origami? You can learn on your own. Plenty of books will give you step-by-step instructions on how to fold a variety of animals, boxes, flowers, and more. Go to the library, and check out a few. Look in the Further Information section at the back of this book for some origami book and website suggestions. Tons of YouTube videos can show you how to fold too. Start with simple designs, and work your way up to more complex ones. Keep your creases precise, and try to improve each time. Keep working at it, and you may start creating your own designs one day!

Here are a few websites to get you going on your origami journey:

OrigamiUSA, an educational and cultural arts organization dedicated to origami and the art of paper folding, has many kinds of origami diagrams available on its site. Choose from a simple cat, a *Brachiosaurus*, an iris, or a sailboat. Find the diagrams here: https://origamiusa.org/diagrams.

Here are two videos by Tom Hull on how to make his PHiZZ units:

PHiZZ Unit Part 1, https://www.youtube.com/watch?v=vFYw47Wx2N8

PHiZZ Unit Part 2, https://www.youtube.com/watch?v=dH-uTRdI4XU

Here's Tom Hull's pattern and instructions for a flapping bat:

http://origametry.net/bat/flapbat.html

For more advanced folders, Robert J. Lang has published some of his crease patterns on his website. They don't come with folding instructions, but a persistent origami artist may be able to figure out the folds. **His crease patterns can be found here:**

https://langorigami.com/crease-patterns/

If you would like to fold from instructions, many of his books contain step-by-step folding instructions. **You can find them here:**

https://langorigami.com/publications/my-books/

being used in the marketplace. And more engineers are realizing the benefits of using folding in their designs. One of the most exciting areas that could benefit from origami is biomedical engineering, which involves engineering tools that can be used for medical purposes inside the human body. "Since origami mechanics work very well at micro-scales," says Hull, "I think [folding] could be very useful in bioengineering. Origami can benefit this area because it can do a lot of interesting mechanical behaviors while at the same time being quite easy to manufacture. Once you have a good origami design, it'll just be made from a flat material, which can be a lot easier to manufacture than, say, actually building a tiny robot from parts."

Biomedical devices inspired by origami are especially appealing to manufacturers because they require few materials and are simple and cheap to make. They're also useful for minimally invasive procedures because the devices can enter a person's body through tiny incisions and either fold or unfold, depending on the device, into their usable forms once inside. Because they need fewer parts to function, these devices are smaller than traditional surgical instruments. Origami scales down well—its folds are the same whether the object is large or small—so it is perfect for creating tiny devices that move without the need for pin joints and other parts. And since these devices can be made cheaply, they are ideal for disposable use.

Researchers have already made several advances in biomedical engineering using origami. At MIT, scientists created a tiny 3D-printable origami robot that could be used inside the body for small surgeries. Made from a heat-induced self-folding plastic sheet and a magnet, the robot measures less than half an inch (1.3 cm) long when folded. To make it move, a person operates electromagnetic coils to create a magnetic field. By changing this field, the robot can walk, move up an incline, lift and carry objects, dig, and swim. It could possibly move to an area of the body to make an incision or deliver drugs. Then, when it is no longer needed, the robot dissolves.

University of Tokyo's Kaori Kuribayashi-Shigetomi, who helped develop the origami heart stent, is using cells to make origami that could deliver drugs to specific areas inside the body. Instead of using plastic as a self-folding material, Kuribayashi-Shigetomi uses living cells and tiny plates made of an environmentally friendly polymer to build 3D structures. This process is called cell origami. The folding mechanism comes from a force within the cells called cell traction force. This force is a kind of tension that is applied to whatever the cells touch and that pulls toward the cells' centers. The force helps cells keep their shape, move, communicate with other cells, and perform other functions. When stretched over two plates, the cells pull toward their center and act as a hinge to the plates. When the plates are laid out in a lowercase T shape, the cell traction force makes the plates fold up into a cube shape. Different plate arrangements create different folded shapes and tubes. Using extracted heart cells, which are cells that contract and relax to make a heart beat, these structures can also move on their own. This cell origami could be used to grow tissues into hollow shapes, make organic robots that move, or package drugs to deliver in the body.

In 2014 BYU developed another microtool, a nanoinjector inspired by *kirigami*, a form of origami that allows cutting as well as folding. The nanoinjector is a tiny lance used on cells. It lays flat and folds up to become a lance that is 1/100th of the width of a human hair. The lance pokes into a cell and then attracts DNA using electrical forces. The lance then extracts the DNA and can deposit it in a new cell, which is useful for research into diseases such as Alzheimer's and diabetes. BYU researchers have already successfully used their nanoinjector on mouse cells. It is a big improvement from current DNA extraction technology that uses needles that harm and kill cells in the process of extraction.

At Penn State University, mechanical and biomedical engineering professor Mary Frecker researches how origami can be used to make better devices and equipment, especially smaller and more efficient tools for surgeons. Frecker says, "If we could have a surgical instrument that could be very small and compact and be inserted into the body through a small incision, say, and then deploy into something larger once inside, then you get all the benefits of the minimally invasive approach." Some of those benefits include less pain to the patient, reduced risk of scarring, quick recovery periods, and shorter hospital stays.

When Frecker's team began designing microtools, they had some challenges working with small hinges and joints, which are essential elements of any mechanical device. They turned to origami for the solution because it uses one folded material to achieve the same movements as those of machines made with several pieces connected by hinges and joints. The devices that her team designs start out as flat sheets that self-fold into different designs. They use a variety of materials that respond to different stimuli, such as force, electricity, or magnetism. When these materials are combined with one another, they respond in different ways—some bend up or down, move forward, or fold into a box. Their research focuses on making better scopes, which thread through a person's body to the site of injury or disease before beginning treatment at the site.

Doctors sometimes use medical scopes to search inside cancer patients' bodies for tumors. Scopes enter the body through a very small opening or cut. A device at the tip of the scope stays packed tightly inside until the scope reaches a tumor. When the scope reaches the tumor, the tip extends from the scope to reach the cancer cells. It heats the cancer cells until they become so damaged that they cannot survive. Previous scope tips could only heat up small points of the tumor, but one device Frecker and her team are working on has a scope tip that unfolds as it approaches the tumor, its ends splaying out like feathers. This tip can heat up a much larger area of the tumor, killing more cancer cells and increasing the patient's chances for getting rid of the tumor. The team wants to improve the tips of these scopes using origami-inspired folding mechanisms that are multifunctional. These tips may be able to cut, grasp, move, and more.

FLYING AND FOLDING: DRONES

People have used unpiloted flying vehicles—drones—since World War II. First, they were fighter pilot practice targets, but with different equipment drones became important military tools and

Follow the Drone

Want to see this drone in action? The University of Zürich Robotics and Perception group has a video of the drone flying in its different configurations. Watch it here: https://www.youtube.com/watch?v=jmKXCdEbF_E/.

weapons in themselves. Using cameras, drones take spy photos and videos, and when armed, they become high-precision weapons. Large military drones can drop missiles, and smaller drones can spy on enemies. Commercial companies and health providers are even using drones to deliver goods and medicines to consumers and patients. Drones may even have another use—as first responders in disaster zones. Folding helps drones get into places no person or robot can.

Inspired by the way birds can change shape while flying and still maintain steady flight, researchers at the University of Zurich have developed the first drone that can fold while in flight. Studies show how pigeons and swifts adapt the surface area of their wings to fly better in different conditions. For instance, pigeons fold their wings in tightly to their bodies to move through small spaces. To mimic this ability, scientists developed a quadrotor—a drone with four propellers. Its four folding arms extend from a central core, each moving independently from the other. This allows the drone to move in three different configurations, each designed to help it enter differently shaped spaces.

The drone's default **X-shaped configuration** allows the drone to maximize flight time and agility. In its **H-shaped configuration**, the drone has two arms forward and two arms backward, allowing it to move through narrow vertical spaces. In its **O-shaped configuration**, the drones' arms are all folded in and equally spaced around the core. This allows it to fly through horizontal spaces. And in a **T-shaped configuration**, two of its arms are folded near the core while two extend to the sides. This lets the drone closely inspect vertical surfaces.

The scientists believe this kind of adaptable folding drone could help during search and rescue missions. After entering tight openings, the drone could explore collapsed buildings too dangerous and unstable for humans to enter. It may even be able to locate survivors and save lives.

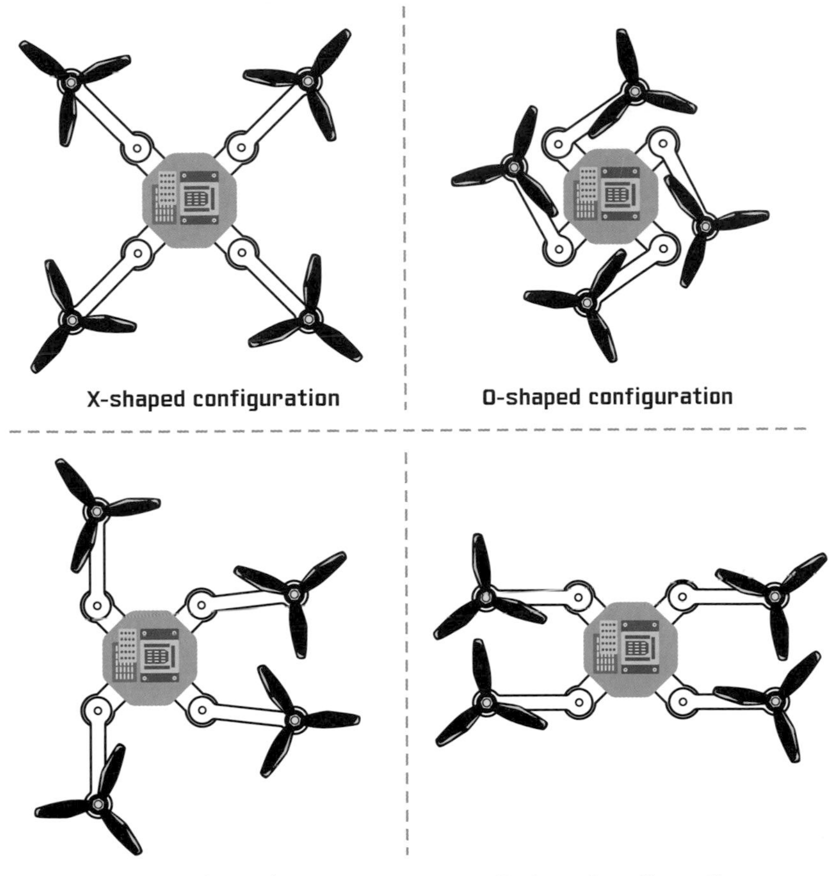

MORPHING ORIGAMI

One new folding pattern could help protect drones if they crash, make music sound better, and much more. The Georgia Institute of Technology engineers who designed this new pattern named it morph. That's because it isn't like regular origami, which can move from flat to folded positions and back again. This new pattern can change (or morph) from one folded pattern to another or even become a hybrid of its two parent patterns. It's a highly adaptable folding pattern that allows structures to change to multiple shapes.

The morph pattern has two parent patterns: the Miura-ori and eggbox patterns. Both parent patterns fold into sheets of repeating shapes. The Miura-ori folds into what looks like rows of zigzag shapes, while the eggbox pattern folds into a series of mountain and valley-like shapes. They both fold flat but curve in different ways when folded into a sheet of tessellations—Miura-ori bends in a dome shape, and the eggbox pattern bends in a saddle shape.

The morph pattern has the ability to bend both ways and even in combination when in its hybrid form. It can do so because of the design of its basic cell. Two planes on one side of the cell are shrunk down from its parent patterns forms. This allows their folds to switch from mountain to valley folds—whether the material being folded is pliable (such as paper) or rigid (such as metal).

Glaucio Paulino, a professor at Georgia Tech School of Civil and Environmental Engineering who's involved with the study on morph, said, "This hybrid origami allows for reprogrammable mechanical properties and the ability to change those properties while the material is in service." That means that a wall could change its function and appearance right before your eyes. A drone's surface could suddenly change shape when about to crash, lessening the overall damage by allowing the drone to absorb more energy from the crash at its surface while protecting its inner components. And an acoustic system on the ceiling of a concert hall could adapt to the kinds of music being played onstage, making it louder or softer or even have other resonant responses based on how the material curves. This mechanical adaptability could make folding technology useful in many imagined and not yet imaginable ways.

STARSHADES AND SOLAR SAILS

Folding is also being used by NASA scientists to design the proposed Starshade, a giant shade that could be used to block light and help telescopes see distant planets outside of our solar system.

This artist's concept shows how the Starshade might align with a space telescope to block a distant star's light so that the telescope can directly image any exoplanets or exomoons orbiting the star. Each petal on the Starshade's "flower" will be coated in a special gold foil that reflects infrared and UV radiation that would otherwise interfere with the telescope's imaging.

The Starshade looks like a giant sunflower, with petals circling a center point. Scientists modeled the shade using the origami iris pattern. The shade would need to pack up tightly into a rocket. To unfold, it has a system of supports that radiate from a central core. The shade's petals curve and overlap around the central core, which then expand as the supports extend around the core. An inner shield then expands, pushing the petals out much farther. When fully expanded, the Starshade would reach the incredible diameter of 85 feet (26 m).

Once deployed, the Starshade could sit directly between a space telescope and a star. The shade would block the star's light, allowing the telescope to see what might be moving around the star, such as planets and their moons. The Starshade will allow the telescope to

Starshade Origami

Do you want to fold your own origami Starshade? NASA has a project online that shows you how to fold a replica of the inner shield of the Starshade. Use your computer to download and print the template on either 11-by-17-inch (28 by 43 cm) or 8.5-by-11-inch (21.5 by 28 cm) paper. The only other tools you need are a scissors and a pen. Follow the instructions on their site to make your miniature origami Starshade!

https://www.jpl.nasa.gov/edu/learn/project/space-origami-make-your-own-starshade/

directly image any exoplanets it finds. Usually telescopes can only indirectly "see" exoplanets by watching the effects the orbiting planets have on a star's light or position. The Starshade mission has not yet been approved for flight by NASA, but its researchers are developing the technologies needed to make this mission happen in the 2020s.

Origami can also help propel engineless spacecraft. The Japan Aerospace Exploration Agency (JAXA) used origami to design solar sails for a spacecraft without engines, called the Interplanetary Kite-craft Accelerated by Radiation Of the Sun (IKAROS), which launched in 2010. The sails rely on sunlight, which is made of tiny particles called photons. Each photon has energy as it moves away from the sun. When a photon hits the sail, it transfers its energy to the sail, causing it to move forward. The sails were folded up tightly while IKAROS was inside its rocket. Then they unfolded when the spacecraft reached space. IKAROS was the first example of origami-inspired solar sails used in space. Since then, the Planetary Society launched CubeSats, a crowdfunded solar sail project that uses solar sails to propel small cube-shaped satellites and spacecraft.

Scientists, artists, designers, and engineers continue to search for ways that origami can benefit technology, art, architecture, and more. Someday the world may be filled with folded technology that

This illustration shows the IKAROS spacecraft as it flies through the solar system. Propelled entirely by sunlight, IKAROS sailed past Venus in December 2010. It continues to orbit the sun but has been in hibernation mode since 2015.

was inspired by nature and origami. Imagine using power beamed down to Earth from solar panels that unfolded from rockets to use in your kitchen that has stowaway countertops and furniture that pops up from the floor. Inside your body, a tiny robot delivers medicine to your heart. Inside your car, an airbag is safely folded up inside your dashboard, ready to deploy when you need it the most. You may never have thought it was possible, but art may inspire the technology that one day saves your life.

SERIOUS ORIGAMI: BECOMING A PROFESSIONAL

What does it take to move from origami hobbyist to professional origamist and mathematician? It's not a conventional career path, and it seems to be different for each person. One thing that professional origamists have in common is a natural interest in origami from an early age. Having a passion for geometry and mathematics helps too. Here's some advice from Hull and Lang.

When it comes to learning math, Hull advises to never give up, even when you can't seem to find the correct answer. That happens often, and Hull believes that math continually shows you how you are wrong, forcing you to keep trying until you are correct. Hull feels lucky to do math and origami through his career as a professor but knows math is a tough field. Passion and persistence are the keys to being successful at it.

If you want to pursue a career in origami engineering, Hull believes students should take lots of math classes. "Math is a huge area, and there is so much to learn," Hull says. "The more math you know, the easier all sorts of other fields in science become, especially engineering and physics. And it is becoming easier for students to find resources on origami and math, or origami and engineering, so students can hunt some of those things down while they're learning lots of math."

The applications of origami vary widely, from technology and advertising to fashion and furniture. Lang says students should "learn a lot about many fields that *might* be applicable [and they] will be better prepared to go into the one that actually turns out to be applicable—and even better [they'll] be prepared to follow the new interdisciplinary field that never existed before." He thinks students should just start folding whatever they enjoy folding, learning from the process, and doing what makes them happy. They should focus on folding well too, using crisp and clean folds, and learning different techniques from books, websites, or videos.

For students in high school, Lang suggests "taking some art classes in which you create art: drawing, sculpture, or other form of art. . . . The things you are seeking to get out of art classes are knowledge and practice of technique: how to look at a subject and create a representation in another medium." Learning digital art and taking some computer programming classes would be helpful too. He suggests taking geometry, algebra, trigonometry, and linear algebra math classes, although they're not necessary for every origami artist.

In college, students can begin to specialize their learning to fit their interests. If they want to work as origami artists, they can go to design and art schools, such as the Rhode Island School of Design, New York City's Cooper Union, or Pasadena's ArtCenter College of Design. If they want to use origami in technology, students can attend a mechanical engineering program. "If you become a mechanical engineer, there will be ample opportunity to bring origami into what you do," Lang says. If students are interested in using origami in artful structures, they can study architecture. Computational geometry is another field of study that blends origami with computer science. "It seems likely to me that many future innovations in design algorithms and the theory of origami will come from the field of computational geometry," Lang says, "and with a solid grounding in computer science, you will be well equipped to pursue them."

Being able to communicate your ideas, projects, and experience well is also very important, so Lang suggests students take English composition or literary criticism classes. They will help students learn how to express themselves through writing, which is important for the business side of being a professional origamist. "Whether you are selling yourself via your website, or working as an industrial designer or a mechanical engineer, or developing unfolding spacecraft for NASA, you are going to be communicating what you do to others," Lang explains. "If you want to be able to fold what you want, you need to be in control of your own destiny, and for that to happen, you need to be able to communicate clearly."

NASA'S FOLDING MACHINES

Origami engineering first took shape in space with Miura's solar array, and space remains one of the places that could benefit the most from folding. With the tight restrictions on rocket size, folding is the ideal solution for many space applications.

PUFFER

Imagine the perfect alien planet scout. It can climb over all kinds of imaginable terrains—snowy hills, desert plains, steep slopes, rolling dunes, or dust-filled Martian craters. But even more incredible is its ability to squeeze into tight crevices and caves to find possible life-forms safely hidden from the harsh elements. NASA is working on a robotic investigator that would be capable of all of this. They call it the Pop-Up Flat Folding Explorer Robot (PUFFER), a machine with a design that was inspired by origami.

A researcher tests PUFFER's maneuverability in below-freezing temperatures. Because the temperature on the surface of Mars can drop to −225°F (−143°C), PUFFER must be able to operate in the extreme cold.

HOW TO USE THE LERNER AR APP

Download the free Lerner AR app on your digital device from the App Store or Google Play. As you read, look for this icon—it means there is an **augmented reality** experience on that page. Use the Lerner AR app to scan the picture near the icon to see folding tech in action!

The Apple logo is a trademark of Apple Inc., registered in the U.S. and other countries and regions. App Store is a service mark of Apple Inc. Google Play and the Google Play logo are trademarks of Google LLC.

Rovers are the main explorers on planetary expeditions, but these larger robots can't go everywhere. A small, flexible, and lightweight PUFFER could assist the rovers with exploring smaller spaces. Its design allows it to flatten completely and stack onto the rover. When ready to use PUFFER, the rover flicks the PUFFER onto the ground. PUFFER unfolds and starts moving across the planet's surface. Robotics electrical engineer Jaakko Karras modeled PUFFER's body using folded circuit boards instead of paper, which allowed him to include electronics such as a control system and scientific instruments in the model. The development team 3D-printed treaded wheels to attach to the body, which can be folded over the body so that the robot can crawl into small spaces. As the design evolved, the team gave PUFFER a tail for stability and added solar panels underneath its body so that it can flip over and power up using the sun's energy.

PUFFER is still in development at NASA's Jet Propulsion Laboratory, but it's the robot's folding tech that makes it especially useful and so unique. On unexplored planets, where scientists hope to one day find life (or evidence of life), the microbots could investigate difficult and dangerous areas too small for a rover to reach. These hidden spots, under overhanging rocks and inside crevices and cracks, may be the perfect environments for alien bacteria and microorganisms. Perhaps PUFFER will be the first to find these alien creatures by folding its body to inch inside their hidden homes.

The InSight Lander

One piece of folding tech is helping scientists on Earth answer questions about Mars—how the planet formed, what its current weather is like, and how its tectonic plates move—and "see" into the planet's core. This tech is on the Interior Exploration using Seismic Investigations, Geodesy and Heat Transport (InSight) lander, which touched down on Mars on November 26, 2018.

Technicians surround InSight as the backshell is connected to the folded lander in the final stages of the spacecraft's construction. The backshell helped protect InSight as it entered Mars's atmosphere in November 2018.

Other landers have studied the surface of Mars—its canyons, volcanoes, rocks, and soil. But InSight is the first to study the planet's interior structure. Mars is one of the four rocky planets in our solar system, and so learning about its structure will help us understand how other rocky planets formed, including Earth. To conduct its many experiments, InSight is equipped with a suite of scientific instruments and a robotic arm to move them from the lander's deck to the ground. And to power everything, the lander has two solar arrays. These arrays were folded up tightly in a fanlike configuration during travel but opened up shortly after landing to create two circular panels, each measuring 7 feet (2.1 m) across, almost the size of a Ping-Pong table. These two arrays can produce 600 to 700 watts of electricity from sunlight on clear days (and only 200 to 300 watts during a dust storm), which is then stored in batteries for the lander to use when needed.

Since landing, InSight has made many firsts on Mars. It recorded the first sounds from Mars—a low rumbling noise made by wind. As a windstorm blew across the lander, two of its sensitive sensors recorded sounds made by the moving air that caused the solar arrays to vibrate. The lander was the first to detect and measure a Marsquake, a kind of planetary shudder caused by its cooling and contraction that creates stress within the planet. The crust cracks to release the stress, which causes the Marsquake.

TIMELINE:
FROM ORIGAMI ART TO SPACE APPLICATIONS

600s: The art of paper folding originates in Japan and is first used for religious and ceremonial purposes.

1603–1867: During Japan's Edo period, paper folding goes mainstream, as paper becomes cheaper to make and buy. People start folding paper for fun.

1797: The oldest known, very simple origami instructions are published in the book *Orikata Tehon Chushingura* by publisher Yoshinoya Tamehachi of Kyoto.

1950s: Origami master Akira Yoshizawa starts gaining worldwide recognition for his uniquely exquisite and original origami designs. His variations on traditional origami designs spread to Western culture.

1954: Akira Yoshizawa publishes his system of dashed and dotted lines and arrows used in origami folding patterns in his book *Atarashii Origami Geijutsu.* This "origami language" allowed people who do not speak Japanese to learn how to fold origami. People in Western cultures start making origami using these kinds of diagrams.

1970s: Koryo Miura begins studying a folding pattern he believes could be useful to aerospace technology.

1980s: Origami theorems are developed by origami mathematics pioneers, including Toshikazu Kawasaki, Koshiro Hatori, Jun Maekawa, Humiaki Huzita, and Jacques Justin.

1985: Miura proposes using his developable double corrugation surface (Miura-ori) pattern for solar arrays.

1989: The First International Meeting of Origami Science and Technology takes place in Ferrara, Italy.

Early 1990s: Multiple artists, including Robert J. Lang, develop mathematical models for complex origami design. Lang creates the TreeMaker computer program, used to design complex pieces of origami.

March 18, 1995: The Space Flyer Unit launches, carrying solar arrays folded in Miura's pattern. The solar panels successfully deploy in space.

2000: Lang works with the Lawrence Livermore National Laboratory to design a space telescope lens.

2012: The Japanese American National Museum shows the very first exhibition highlighting the connections between origami, math, science, and design, called *Folding Paper: The Infinite Possibilities of Origami*.

2012 and 2013: The National Science Foundation (NSF) awards thirteen grants for research projects that focused on Origami Design for Integration of Self-assembling Systems for Engineering Innovation (ODISSEI). Researchers have used NSF funds and other resources to develop a wide array of origami and nature-inspired folding technology—from heart stents to Starshades—many of which are still in the developmental stage.

2017: NASA scientists create the Pop-Up Flat Folding Explorer Robot (PUFFER), a robotic mini-rover that folds and unfolds based on origami design principles.

May 2018: University of Tokyo researchers uncover the folding patterns of ladybug wings by conducting an experiment using a transparent elytron. They find a springlike action in its veins, which could help researchers develop folding aircraft wings and better umbrellas.

April 2019: Georgia Institute of Technology engineers create the morph pattern, which can move from flat to folded positions and back again and change (or morph) from one folded pattern to another or even become a hybrid of its two parent patterns. This highly adaptable folding pattern allows structures to have multiple shapes.

GLOSSARY

algorithms: step-by-step instructions used by computers to solve complex problems

axioms: unprovable rules that are accepted as true because they are self-evident or especially useful

biomimetics: the study of the structure, formation, or function of naturally formed objects, substances, or materials in order to artificially recreate them for human use

cell origami: the use of the natural pulling force of a cell to make it fold into 3D structures using other cells and materials

computational biologists: scientists who use biological data to create algorithms for computer programs

computational origami: the study of computer algorithms to solve paper-folding problems

corrugated: having alternating ridges and grooves

Delian problem: the ancient Greek mathematical problem concerning how to double the volume of a cube

designer proteins: cell proteins designed by scientists in laboratories that have enhanced functions

elytra: the hard forewings of beetles that protect their delicate hind wings folded underneath

Fibonacci sequence: a numerical sequence in which each number is the sum of the preceding two numbers

microscale: at a very small or microscopic scale

Miura-ori: the folding pattern created by Koryo Miura that was first used on a deployable solar panel experiment aboard the Space Flyer Unit

mountain fold: a creased fold where the crease points up and the fold opens down

neurons: cells that are part of the nervous system and that transfer messages to and from the brain

origami: the Japanese art form using folding to change paper squares into representational forms and sculptures

origami engineering: structural engineering that uses folding techniques inspired by origami

origamist: a professional artist who uses origami to create art

prefabricated: factory-manufactured sections of a structure that can be quickly assembled into a building

proteins: substances found in cells that are made of amino acids and that tell the cell how to function

prototype: a first model of an object that is used as a pattern for later copies of that object

resilin: an elastic substance found in insects, especially within the hinges and ligaments of their wings

rigid origami: a branch of origami that uses flat, stiff sheets of materials joined by hinges to make the materials fold

self-folding: to fold on its own, with little to no outside pressure

Shinto: an ancient Japanese religion that consists of devotions to gods of natural forces and the worship of the emperor as a descendant of the sun goddess

simulation: the production of a computer model of something so that it can be studied

tessellation: a pattern made by a repeated shape that does not have any gaps in between the shapes

valley fold: a creased fold where the crease points down and the fold opens up

SOURCE NOTES

24 Robert J. Lang, author interview, July 17, 2018.

24 Lang.

26 Lang.

26 Lang.

26 Lang.

27 Lang.

38 Kayla Wiles, "Origami Folds of Insect Wing Can Help Improve Machine Functions," Purdue University news release,March 22, 2018, https://www.purdue.edu/newsroom/releases/2018/Q1/origami-folds-of-insect-wing-can-help-improve-machine-functions.html.

39 Mihai Andrei, "Scientists Create Earwig-Inspired Origami, with Potential Applications in Space Travel, Foldable Electronics, and Tents," *ZME Science*, March 23, 2018, https://www.zmescience.com/science/news-science/earwig-origami-space-folds-22032018/.

39 Jason Daley, "The Origami-Like Folds of Ladybug Wings Could Lead to Better Umbrellas," *Smithsonian Magazine*, May 19, 2017, https://www.smithsonianmag.com/smart-news/folding-ladybug-wings-could-lead-better-solar-panels-and-umbrellas-180963379/.

41 Kazuya Saito, et al., "Investigation of Hindwing Folding in Ladybird Beetles by Artificial Elytron Transplantation and Microcomputed Tomography," *PNAS* 114, no. 22 (May 30, 2017): 5624–5628, https://www.pnas.org/cgi/doi/10.1073/pnas.1620612114.

42 Bryson Masse, "Your Umbrella May Be Getting an Upgrade Thanks to Ladybug Wings," *Gizmodo*, May 15, 2017, https://gizmodo.com/your-umbrella-may-be-getting-an-upgrade-thanks-to-ladyb-1795227111/.

47 Lang, interview.

47 Thomas Hull, author interview, August 17, 2018.

48–49 Hull.

50 David Huffman, "Curvature and Creases: A Primer on Paper," *IEEE Transactions on Computers* 25, no. 10 (October 1976), http://www.organicorigami.com/thrackle/class/hon394/papers/HuffmanCurvatureAndCreases.pdf.

50 S. A. Robertson, "Isometric Folding of Riemannian Manifolds," *Proceedings of the Royal Society of Edinburgh Section A: Mathematics* 79, no. 3–4 (1978): 275–284, https://doi.org/10.1017/S0308210500019788.

54 Hull, interview, September 11, 2018.

54 Hull.

54 Hull.

55 Hull.

55–56 Hull, interview, August 17, 2018.

57 Hull.

59 Hull.

64 Jason S. Ku and Erik D. Demaine, "Folding Flat Crease Patterns with Thick Materials," *Journal of Mechanisms and Robotics* 8, no. 3 (June 2016), http://jasonku.mit.edu/pdf/THICKFOLDING_JMR.pdf.

67 Hull, interview, August 17, 2018

67 Zeeya Merali, "Origami Engineer Flexes to Create Stronger, More Agile Materials," *Science* 332, no. 6036 (June 17, 2011): 1376–1377.

71 Merali, 1377.

76 Hull, interview, August 17, 2018.

78 "Science of Innovation: Origami Structures," NBC News video, 5:54, February 11, 2016, https://www.nbclearn.com/science-of-innovation/cuecard/105467/.

82 Georgia Institute of Technology, "Morphing Origami Takes a New Shape, Expanding Use Possibilities," Phys.org, April 17, 2019, https://phys.org/news/2019-04-morphing-origami-possibilities.html.

86 Hull, interview, August 17, 2018.

86 Lang, "Careers in Origami," *Fold* 22 (May/June 2014), https://origamiusa.org/thefold/article/careers-origami/.

86 Lang.

87 Lang.

87 Lang.

87 Lang.

SELECTED BIBLIOGRAPHY

Faber, Jakob A., Andres F. Arrieta, and André R. Studart. "Bioinspired Spring Origami." *Science* 359, no. 6382: 1386–1391. https://doi.org/10.1126/science.aap7753.

Forbes, Peter. *The Gecko's Foot: Bio-inspiration—Engineering New Materials from Nature*. New York: W. W. Norton, 2005.

Hardesty, Larry. "Shape-Shifting Robots." Massachusetts Institute of Technology, August 5, 2010. http://news.mit.edu/2010/programmable-matter-0805/.

Holland, Jennifer S. "Fold Everything." *National Geographic* 216, no. 4 (October 2009): 24–27.

Hull, Thomas. *Project Origami: Activities for Exploring Mathematics*. 2nd ed. Boca Raton, FL: CRC, 2013.

Kenneway, Eric. *Complete Origami: An A–Z of Facts and Folds, with Step-by-Step Instruction for over 100 Projects*. New York: St. Martin's, 1987.

Kobayashi, H., Biruta Kresling, and J. V. F. Vincent. "The Geometry of Unfolding Tree Leaves." *Proceedings of the Royal Society of London: Biological Sciences* 265, no. 1391 (January 1998): 147–154.

Kresling, Biruta. "Natural Twist Buckling in Shells: From the Hawkmoth's Bellows to the Deployable Kresling-Pattern and Cylindrical Miura-Ori." *Deployable Structures and Biological Morphology*. Internet-First University Press, 2010. https://ecommons.cornell.edu/handle/1813/11530.

Ku, Jason S., and Erik Demaine. "Folding Flat Crease Patterns with Thick Materials." *Journal of Mechanisms and Robotics* 8, no. 3 (June 2016). http://jasonku.mit.edu/pdf/THICKFOLDING_JMR.pdf.

Kuribayashi-Shigetomi, Kaori. "Folding the Future with Origami." YouTube video, 18:31. Posted by TEDx Talks, August 25, 2016. https://www.youtube.com/watch?v=Dg2XLtUJQFM/.

Lang, Robert J. *Origami Design Secrets: Mathematical Methods for an Ancient Art*. 2nd ed. Boca Raton, FL: CRC, 2011.

———. Robert J. Lang Origami. Accessed April 30, 2020. http://langorigami.com.

———. *Twists, Tilings, and Tesselations: Mathematical Methods for Geometric Origami*. Boca Raton, FL: CRC, 2018.

Mackenzie, Dana, and Barry Cipra. "Origami: Unfolding the Future." In *What's Happening in the Mathematical Sciences?* Vol. 10. Providence, RI: American Mathematical Society, 2010.

Merali, Zeeya. "Origami Engineer Flexes to Create Stronger, More Agile Materials." *Science* 332, no. 6036 (June 17, 2011): 1376–1377.

Miura, Koryo. "Method of Packaging and Deployment of Large Membranes in Space." *Institute of Space and Astronautical Science* 618 (December 1985). https://repository.exst.jaxa.jp/dspace/bitstream/a-is/7293/1/SA0035000.pdf.

Miura, Koryo, Toshikazu Kawasaki, Tomohiro Tachi, Ryuhei Uehara, and Robert J. Lang, eds. *Origami 6: Mathematics*. Providence, RI: American Mathematical Society, 2015.

Miyashita, Shuhei, Steven Guitron, Marvin Ludersdorfer, Cynthia R. Sung, and Daniela Rus. "An Untethered Miniature Origami Robot That Self-Folds, Walks, Swims, and Degrades." International Conference on Robotics and Automation, May 2015. https://dspace.mit.edu/handle/1721.1/97147.

Morgan, David C., Denise M. Halverson, Spencer P. Magleby, Terri C. Bateman, and Larry L. Howell. *Y Origami? Explorations in Folding*. Providence, RI: American Mathematical Society, 2017.

Neznanova, Anastassiya, and Shenglan Yuan. "From Ancient Greece to Beloch's Crease: The Delian Problem and Origami." *International Journal of Undergraduate Research and Creative Activities 7* (February 2015): 3. http://dx.doi.org/10.7710/2168-0620.1042.

"Origami-Paper Folding and Its Generalization—Tomohiro Tachi, the University of Tokyo." Vimeo video, 28:10. Posted by Kavli Frontiers of Science, February 6, 2015. https://vimeo.com/118974216/.

Rehmeyer, Julie J. "Mathematical Lives of Plants: Why Plants Grow in Geometrically Curious Patterns." *Science News* 172, no. 3 (May 7, 2007). https://www.sciencenews.org/article/mathematical-lives-plants/.

Saitoa, Kazuya, Shuhei Nomurab, Shuhei Yamamotoc, Ryuma Niiyamad, and Yoji Okabea. "Investigation of Hindwing Folding in Ladybird Beetles by Artificial Elytron Transplantation and Microcomputed Tomography," *PNAS* 114, no. 22 (May 30, 2017): 5624–5628. https://www.pnas.org/cgi/doi/10.1073/pnas.1620612114.

Schmidt, Petra, and Nicola Stattmann. *Unfolded: Paper in Design, Art, Architecture and Industry*. Basel, Switzerland: Birkhäuser Architecture, 2009.

Singh, Parmanand. "The So-Called Fibonacci Numbers in Ancient and Medieval India." *Historia Mathematica* 12, no. 3 (August 1985): 229–244.

Smith, C. W., D. S. A. De Focatiis, and S. D. Guest. "Deployable Membranes Designed from Folding Tree Leaves." *Philosophical Transactions of the Royal Society of London: Mathematical, Physical and Engineering Sciences* 360, no. 1791 (January 11, 2002). https://royalsocietypublishing.org/doi/10.1098/rsta.2001.0928.

Teoh, Z. E., B. T. Phillips, K. P. Becker, G. Whittredge, J. C. Weaver, C. Hoberman, D. F. Gruber, and R. J. Wood. "Rotary-Actuated Folding Polyhedrons for Midwater Investigation of Delicate Marine Organisms." *Science Robotics* 3, no. 2 (July 18, 2018). https://robotics.sciencemag.org/content/robotics/3/20/eaat5276.full.pdf.

Wiles, Kayla. "Origami Folds of Insect Wing Can Help Improve Machine Functions." Purdue University, March 22, 2018. https://www.purdue.edu/newsroom/releases/2018/Q1/origami-folds-of-insect-wing-can-help-improve-machine-functions.html.

FURTHER INFORMATION

"Careers in Origami"
https://origamiusa.org/thefold/article/careers-origami/
This article by Robert J. Lang tells readers how to pursue a career as a professional origamist, from courses to take in school and college to the stamina and communication skills needed to succeed in this unique profession.

"Cool Jobs: The Art of Paper Folding Is Inspiring Science"
https://www.sciencenewsforstudents.org/article/cool-jobs-paper-folding-origami-inspiring-science/
This article by Rachel Crowell features different scientists and engineers using origami to guide their technological designs and art and discusses the work and research they are doing in this field.

Five Intersecting Tetrahedra
http://origametry.net/fit.html

Koch, Melissa. *3D Printing: The Revolution in Personalized Manufacturing*. Minneapolis: Lerner Publications. 2018.
Discover how 3D printing, used to create materials for some folding technologies, has revolutionized manufacturing.

"The Math and Magic of Origami"
https://www.ted.com/talks/robert_lang_folds_way_new_origami/
Watch origami master Robert J. Lang explain some of the mathematical principles and artistry behind modern origami sculptures in this TED talk.

Origami-Make.org
http://www.origami-make.org/
Visit this site to learn the basic folds of origami. The site features a large selection of models with step-by-step instructions.

The Origami Revolution
https://www.pbs.org/wgbh/nova/video/the-origami-revolution/
Watch this PBS documentary to see how the ancient art of origami is inspiring scientists and engineers to create high-tech solutions to problems inside human bodies, on Earth, and in space.

Pentagon-Hexagon Zig-Zag Unit (PHiZZ)
http://origametry.net/phzig/phzig.html
Visit these links to learn how to make Thomas Hull's famous modular origami designs.

Trebbi, Jean-Charles, Chloe Genevaux, and Guillaume Bounoure. *The Art of Folding Volume 2: New Trends, Techniques, and Materials*. Barcelona: Promopress Editions, 2017.
This book presents a variety of creators who work with different materials and are inspired by origami and nature, making structures, fashion, furniture, lighting, and more.

Yoshizawa, Akira, Kazuo Hamada, Kiyo Yoshizawa, and Robert J. Lang. *Akira Yoshizawa, Japan's Greatest Origami Master*. Rutland, VT: Tuttle, 2016.
Learn about the father of modern origami, Akira Yoshizawa, in this book that also contains diagrams for you to try at home.

INDEX

PHOTO ACKNOWLEDGMENTS

Image credits: Yarro Aroon/Shutterstock.com, p. 2; Alexandra Lande/Shutterstock.com, p. 10; NASA/ Chris Gunn (CC BY 2.0), p. 11; NASA, p. 13; Amy Salveson/Independent Picture Service, pp. 14–15, 21, 31 (large outlined crane) (unfolded crease pattern), 41, 44, 51, 52, 53, 64, 81; The Miriam and Ira D. Wallach Division of Art, Prints and Photographs: Print Collection, The New York Public Library. "Lady with paper and scissors, holding origami" New York Public Library Digital Collections, p. 18; prapass/Shutterstock.com, p. 19; Frederic REGLAIN/Gamma-Rapho/Getty Images, p. 20; Photo courtesy of Robert J. Lang pp. 23, 27; Wyss Institute at Harvard University, p. 28; Origamidesigner/ Wikimedia Commons (CC BY 3.0), pp. 30–31; Mr.B-king/Shutterstock.com, p. 35; Dr. Jakob Faber, ETH Zürich, pp. 37, 38; symbiot/Shutterstock.com, p. 40; Anna Benczur/Wikimedia Commons (CC BY-SA 4.0), p. 49; AP Photo/The Republican, Don Treeger, p. 55; SofieLayla Thal/Pixabay CC0, p. 61; NASA/JPL-Caltech/BYU, p. 62; funkyplayer/Shutterstock.com, p. 66; © Z. E. Teoh, B. T. Phillips, K. P. Becker, G. Whittredge, J. C. Weaver, C. Hoberman, D. F. Gruber, R. J. Wood, Rotary-actuated folding polyhedrons for midwater investigation of delicate marine organisms. Sci. Robot. 3, eaat5276 (2018) via Copyright Clearance Center, p. 69; PhonlamaiPhoto/iStock/Getty Images, p. 70; University of Zurich, p. 79; NASA/JPL-Caltech, p. 83; Andrzej Mirecki/Wikimedia Commons (CC BY-SA 3.0), p. 85; © Dylan Taylor, p. 88; NASA/JPL-Caltech/Lockheed Martin, p. 90. Design elements: MicroOne/ Shutterstock.com; Quietword/Shutterstock.com; TarapongS/iStock/Getty Images.

Cover: NASA/JPL-Caltech/BYU (solar panel array); Infinite ideas/500px/Getty Images (ladybug); MicroOne/Shutterstock.com (origami folded letters). Design elements: TarapongS/iStock/Getty Images; Quietword/Shutterstock.com.

ABOUT THE AUTHOR

Karen Latchana Kenney writes books about science for children and young adults. She is especially drawn to creating books about nature, conservation, and groundbreaking scientific discoveries. Her award-winning and star-reviewed books include *Exoplanets: Worlds beyond Our Solar System*, *Everything World War I*, and *Stephen Hawking: Extraordinary Theoretical Physicist*. She lives in Minnesota with her husband and son, and bikes, hikes, and gazes at the night sky in northern Minnesota any moment she can. Visit her online at http://latchanakenney.wordpress.com.